IMAGES
of America

EDENTON AND CHOWAN COUNTY

NORTH CAROLINA

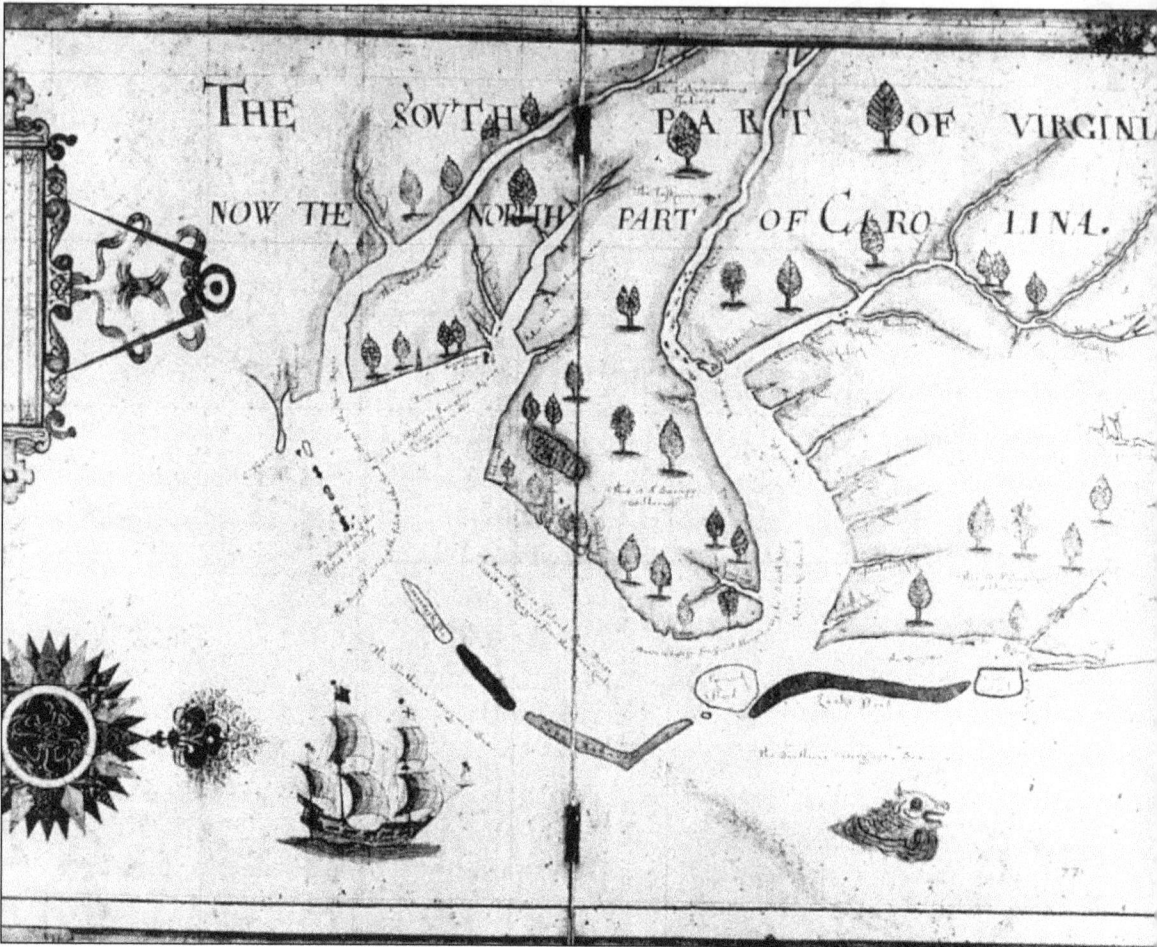

This map drawn by Nicholas Comberford in 1657 shows the location of the Nathaniel Batts house at the fork of the Chowan and Roanoke Rivers. Nathaniel Batts was a young fur trader from Chesapeake Bay, Virginia, who first came to the mouth of the Chowan River in 1653. Batts returned again in 1660 and bought land from the Yeopim Indians. In 1665 he brought workers from Virginia and built a one-room log house. Batts is believed to be the first permanent white settler in North Carolina. Batts traveled by water to widely scattered points which have been named in his honor, such as Batts Island near Hertford, Batts Point on the Pamlico River, and Batts Creek on the Neuse River. Batts is also believed to be a descendant of Margaret Ella Batts Van Camp. (Courtesy of NCDAH.)

On the cover: The Edenton Academy (*c.* 1895) boys baseball team entertains the female students who have gathered to watch in 1907 (see page 77 for more information on Edenton Academy). (Courtesy of SPML.)

2

IMAGES
of America

EDENTON AND CHOWAN COUNTY
NORTH CAROLINA

Louis Van Camp

ARCADIA
PUBLISHING

Published by Arcadia Publishing
Charleston, South Carolina

Library of Congress Catalog Card Number: 2001091446

For all general information contact Arcadia Publishing at:
Telephone 843-853-2070
Fax 843-853-0044
E-mail sales@arcadiapublishing.com
For customer service and orders:
Toll-Free 1-888-313-2665

Visit us on the Internet at www.arcadiapublishing.com

This book is dedicated to all the hardworking families of Chowan County who strive to preserve their heritage, while moving forward in the 21st century.

The Confederate Navy built an ironclad ship named the *Albemarle* at Edward's Ferry in 1864. The Albemarle, commanded by Capt. James W. Cooke, escaped the Union blockade on April 19, 1864, and sank the Union gunboat *Southfield*. The *Albemarle* supported Confederate troops under the command of Gen. Robert F. Hoke during the recapture of Plymouth. On May 5, 1864, the Union gunboat *Sassacus* in an Albemarle Sound naval battle rammed the *Albemarle*, but it escaped with some damage and returned to Plymouth for repairs. A Union night torpedo attack led by Lt. William B. Cushing sank the *Albemarle* at the Plymouth dock on October 26, 1864. (Courtesy NCDAH.)

CONTENTS

In 1755 Joseph Hewes (1730–1779) arrived in Edenton from New Jersey. Hewes was a merchant and a colonial leader. He owned a shipyard along Edenton Bay in the small cove formed by the present junction of Granville and Blount Streets. Hewes was one of the signers of the Declaration of Independence, and was Secretary of the Naval Affairs Committee of the Continental Congress from 1774 to 1777. A monument in his honor is located at the south end of the Town Green. (Courtesy of HESHS.)

INTRODUCTION

The first historical reference to the area now called Edenton and Chowan County was made by Capt. Arthur Barlowe while traveling with Sir Walter Raleigh's first Virginia expedition in 1584. Barlowe raved about the "abundance of waterfowl" along the waters now called Albemarle Sound.

The earliest eastern North Carolina settlers came from Jamestown Island around 1652. Chowan County was originally called Chowan Precinct. This name was derived from the Chowanoc Indians and meant the "people of the south" who live along the Chowan River. In 1696, the English formed the "great county of Bath" which was named in honor of John Granville, Earl of Bath and Palatine of the Province of Carolina. Chowan Precinct (now Chowan County) was located in the heart of the county of Bath.

The parish of St. Paul's was formed in 1701, and "the town on Queen Anne's Creek" was established as a courthouse site in 1712. Edenton was incorporated in 1722, in honor of Colonial Gov. Charles Eden and served as the unofficial capital of the colony until 1746 when the Colonial governor's office was moved to New Bern.

Edenton is bordered by the Chowan River on the west and Edenton Bay on the south edge of the Albemarle Sound. In the 1700s Edenton prospered as the headquarters of Port Roanoke, the Colonial customs district for the west end of Albemarle Sound. Francis Corbin, Lord Granville's land agent, was sent from England in 1744 to administer the port and collect taxes on Lord Granville's property, which extended across the northern half of the English colony. By 1776 the town had a population of 1,000. Edenton prospered during the Revolution because the British were unable to blockade Roanoke Inlet, Edenton's direct outlet to the high seas. After the war, however, two serious problems plagued the town. First, a severe storm in 1795 closed Roanoke Inlet. This closure forced cargo ships to make a longer 130-mile run to Ocracoke Inlet often, against the prevailing southerly wind. The second problem was the opening of the Dismal Swamp Canal from Norfolk in 1805. The canal offered a shortcut to the Virginia trade market, but the sailing vessels had too much draft to run the canal and were not equipped with motor propulsion. However, the shallow draft steamboats could now travel directly from Norfolk to Elizabeth City which was about 70 miles closer than Edenton. To counter these problems local planters invested in such businesses as rope making and large fisheries, but the economy of Edenton still waned. The arrival of the Edenton and Plymouth Steamboat Company vessel *Albemarle* in 1818 gave Edenton an exciting new connection with Norfolk and other Albemarle towns.

By 1850 Edenton was a bustling town of merchants, lawyers, carpenters, cabinetmakers, bricklayers, and sailors. It even had a wigmaker and a silversmith. The 1860 census showed a population of some 900 blacks and 600 whites. Most of the blacks worked as artisans, fishermen, laborers, and servants.

THE WAR BETWEEN THE STATES: 1861–1865

Chowan county residents chose William E. Bond, a Unionist representative, to attend a state secession convention in March of 1861. However, the Union attack at Fort Sumter, South Carolina in April 1861, and Lincoln's call for troops quickly made Secessionists out of all of North Carolina's Unionist leaders. North Carolina seceded from the Union on May 20, 1861. Many residents fled the town in 1862 when Edenton fell to the Union Army. Roanoke Island (and its important inlet) fell to the Union Navy on February 8, 1862. Four days later Union gunboats sailed into Edenton Bay to secure the town.

THE 1865 POST-WAR EFFECT

Edenton was spared physical damage during the Civil War. However, the post-war aftermath resulted in a general economic depression. Local merchants, planters, and fishery owners lost most of their wealth, as well as their slaves. Recovery began in 1866, with the reorganization of the Albemarle Steam Navigation Company, which established a much-needed water connection with railroads to the north. Edenton residents quickly improved their harbor and expanded their local fisheries. On December 15, 1881, the Elizabeth City and Norfolk Railroad arrived in Edenton. By 1892 most of the waterfront had become a huge rail yard. There was a 750-foot pier built to berth the *John W. Garrett*. The *Garrett*, a ship outfitted with tracks, could ferry train cars to the south shore of the Albemarle Sound and land at Mackey's Ferry near Pleasant Grove in Washington County. From Mackey's Depot the main line ran west to Plymouth. A southern spur ran to Belhaven, and a southeast line connected with Roper, Creswell, and Columbia.

By 1907, the line had been completed from Plymouth to Washington, Chocowinity, and Aurora in Beaufort County and ended at Parmele in Craven County. Tons of local fish, cotton, grain, vegetables, and forest naval stores were railroaded north from these counties, and other merchandise was brought back.

In the early 1880s industry grew rapidly. Sawmills were built along the waterfront, the largest of which was the Branning Manufacturing Company's saw and planning mill. In 1893 a fire devastated the wooden storefronts of the downtown "Cheapside" 300 block—a nostalgic replica of the Cheapside District of London. This block was rebuilt with brick buildings in 1894.

By 1898 local investors had formed the Edenton Cotton Mill. The Edenton Peanut Company was formed in 1909. Both companies were located along the railroad track at the eastern edge of town. Edenton's population jumped to 3,000 between 1880 and 1900.

TWENTIETH-CENTURY CHOWAN COUNTY

Twentieth-century Edenton was said to have North Carolina's most prestigious collection of eighteenth-century buildings. For example, the Cupola House at 408 South Broad Street was built in 1758 for Francis Corbin, Lord Granville's land agent. The Cupola House is considered to be one of the finest wooden Jacobean-type houses in the United States. A Historic Edenton and Chowan County Guide Book is available at the Barker House and the Edenton Visitors Center. This booklet illustrates 71 historic properties.

PICTURE CREDIT ABBREVIATIONS

CCAC	Chowan County Arts Council
CCH	Chowan County Herald
ECCC	Edenton and Chowan Chamber of Commerce
EFD	Edenton Fire Department
HESHS	Historic Edenton State Historic Site
MMNV	Mariners Museum of Newport Virginia
NCDAH	North Carolina Department of Archives and History
N&SRR	Norfolk and Southern Railroad
PNC	Preservation, North Carolina
SPML	Shepard-Pruden Memorial Library

One

THE EDENTON WATERFRONT
1701–1960

Scene on Queen Ann's Creek, Edenton, N. C.

Ralph Lane, the leader of the second Raleigh expedition in 1585, proclaimed the land adjoining Queen Anne's Creek to be "the goodliest soile [sic] under the cope of heaven." However, efforts to colonize at that time ended in failure. Around 1650, Englishmen from Virginia began settling this region, which was part of King Charles II's land grant to the Lords Proprieters. By 1701 St. Paul's Parish had been established. This parish town along the shores of Queen Anne's Creek, located on Hayes farm, was renamed Edenton in 1722 in honor of Colonial Gov. Charles Eden. Edenton served as the unofficial colonial capital of the Province of Carolina until 1746 when the Colonial Governor's office was moved to New Bern. Edenton has been poetically described as "the little towne on Queen Anne's Creek." Notice the timber rafts waiting to be floated to a local saw mill in 1915. (Courtesy of HESHS.)

Seine fishing was the only profitable industry in Chowan County during the early 1700s and 1800s. The 1850 census listed 15 fisheries with a capital net worth of $52,500. They employed 500 "free" black men and 127 black women. These fisheries produced 75,375 barrels of fish per season which sold for $62,600, for an investment return of 119 percent. However, the 1860 census showed only five fisheries remaining in Chowan County which then employed only 187 "free" black men and 70 black women. They produced 3,931 barrels of shad and herring which sold for $21,941, for an investment return of 84 percent. Of additional interest is the fact that these fisheries produced their crops during a 10-week fishing season. Their income return was about twice that of all other Edenton industries combined which worked 12 months a year. By 1900 the waters of the Albemarle Sound and Chowan River were over fished, and the industry declined. Of the five remaining fisheries, Ed Hassell's Greenfield Fishery was the largest.

Empty side-wheel platform boats prepare to load the net. (Courtesy of SPML.)

A seine was a long vertical fishing net attached to a guy wire. From the surface it could be dropped as deep as 24 yards. The net was strung between a guy wire on top, which had floats, and a bottom rope, which had sinkers. The fish were caught by drawing the ends of the net together. The nets used in the 1700s and 1800s were sometimes two miles long. It took a large crew of strong men to prepare, launch, and recover the seine. A second crew was employed to sort and barrel the thousands of shad and herring for shipment each day. "Refuse" fish were sold locally and eaten by the fisherman and plantation slaves. A good haul landed up to 90,000 fish, and often six hauls were made a day. Each workman was paid about $1 per day. Frank Baldwin took these pictures in 1903 at the Greenfield Fishery near Edenton. (Courtesy of SPML.)

In this scene workmen were adding cork floats, spaced about a foot apart, to the guy wire. The white man on the left was Mr. George Gilliam Sr. of Halifax, North Carolina. (Courtesy of SPML.)

The seine net was dipped into a tarring pit, which was located between the end of the fishery lane and Capt. Jep Goodwin's house. On the left side of the tar pit was Joe Skinner. (Courtesy of SPML.)

Two steam-powered side-wheel platform boats were used to stretch the long seine net across the sound. (Courtesy of SPML)

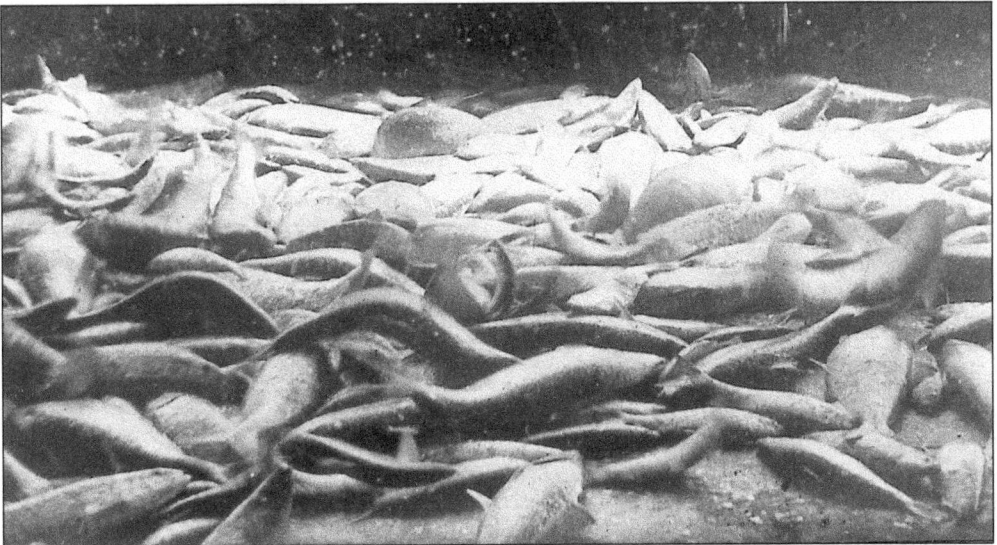

This was a small haul. A large haul netted as many as 90,000 herring and other fish. Up to six hauls were made each day. (Courtesy SPML.)

Before the herring were packed in brine, the heads and tails were removed and the fish were cleaned. (Courtesy of SPML.)

The U.S. Bureau of Fish and Fisheries built the Edenton Fish Hatchery in 1899. It was located on 15 acres of land edging on marshland that is now identified as 705 West Queen Street. This 1901 photo shows, from left to right, the Hatchery building c. 1899, the wooden water tank c. 1900, the pump house (in front) c. 1900, and the superintendent's residence built in 1900. This hatchery became the primary federal source for upgrading vital fishing stock for the Albemarle Sound area. (Courtesy of HESHS.)

Edmund R. Conger (1857–1943) and his wife, Hattie Gillingham Conger (1861–1941), came to Edenton in 1900. Conger started the Edenton Ice and Cold Storage Company along with partners James A. Woolard Jr., William O. Elliott, and William D. Pruden Sr. in 1901. This building was located along the waterfront, which extended toward the channel, "255 feet long, and 66 feet wide . . . which formed a dock . . . that made a complete harbor for small vessels," reported *The Fisherman and Farmer*. (Courtesy of CCH.)

The Edenton-Plymouth-Colerain ferry, pictured in 1920, was operated by B.G. Willis and his son Bert. From 1900 to 1927 they carried passengers and light freight up the Chowan River to Colerain in Bertie County, and to Plymouth in Washington County. In 1927 the first wooden vehicular bridge was built across the Chowan River. (Courtesy of Evelyn Willis.)

Emmitt Wiggins's (1910–1990) cargo boat is pictured waiting to be loaded with watermelons at the county dock in 1935. Chowan County has long been a major producer of watermelons and peanuts. (Courtesy of CCAC.)

16

The Rev. Dr. Robert B. Drane (1851–1939) and his wife, Maria Louisa Skinner Warren Drane (1859–1921), had a 27-foot Chesapeake Bay Skipjack that they and their family enjoyed sailing in Edenton Bay. Dr. Drane was rector of St. Paul's Episcopal Church from 1876 to 1932. (Courtesy of Francis Inglis and SPML.)

William C. Waff (1865–1949) and his wife, Lula Wilson Waff (1868–1939), pose with daughter Myrtle Lou Waff and family friends aboard their motor skiff *Letters* in 1915. William is on the fore deck with his hand on the cabin top. Lula is sitting behind the post, and Myrtle is in a white dress sitting next to her. The other passengers are unknown. The Waff family had a charming Victorian cottage at 209 Court Street, built in 1905. (Courtesy of CCAC.)

John W. and Clarence Branning of Pennsylvania established the Branning Manufacturing Company in 1888. Branning built mills on both sides of Filbert's Creek. The Norfolk and Southern Railroad immediately provided a spur to the plant. By 1899 Branning was shipping 75,000 feet of plane lumber daily. In 1910 Branning sold the mills to M.G. Brown and Company who continued operating on a smaller scale until around 1950. The Brown Lumber Company still operates at the Albania site on West Queen Street. This pastel by E.N. Smith shows the Albania Mill with an old fish house on the left. (Courtesy of Patsy Collins.)

This three-masted cargo schooner was a throwback to the late 1800s. It came to Edenton not under sail but by diesel propulsion in 1959 to pick up some produce cargo. Sailing ships like these transported lumber from the mills in the 1800s. However, the railroad offered the mills quicker and cheaper transport. By 1915 most of these majestic "dragons of the wind" were out of business. (Courtesy of CCAC)

Two

THE ARRIVAL OF THE
RAILROAD IN 1881

The Elizabeth City & Norfolk Railroad came to Edenton on December 13, 1881. By 1883 the waterfront train yard and wharf had been completed on Blount Street. That same year the EC&NRR was renamed the Norfolk and Southern Railroad, and the waterfront soon developed into a huge complex. In 1889 a passenger depot and a 750-foot pier were added to the Blount Street rail yard—the pier built to berth the 364-by-73 foot *John W. Garrett*. This "queen of the bay," with a dining room and elaborate staterooms, ferried 24-train cars from Waddill across the Albemarle Sound to Mackey's Ferry landing. In 1904 the N&SRR purchased the Washington and Plymouth Railroad and extended that rail line to Mackey's Ferry. The *Garrett* operated until 1910 when the N&SRR railroad trestle was completed between Waddill and Mackey's landing. After 188 years of settlement Edenton had its first land connection with neighboring southern counties. Now, the southern counties could ship products by a shorter route to Virginia markets. In 1908 the Norfolk Southern Railroad built a passenger station on East Queen Street; it was demolished in 1970. This July 4, 1915 scene shows cars parked while the owners await the arrival of the Daylight Express train from Norfolk. (Courtesy of N&SRR.)

By 1893 the Norfolk and Southern Railroad's Blount Street rail yard complex was complete. The *John W. Garrett* loaded its train cars at the dock shown on the right. (Courtesy of N&SRR.)

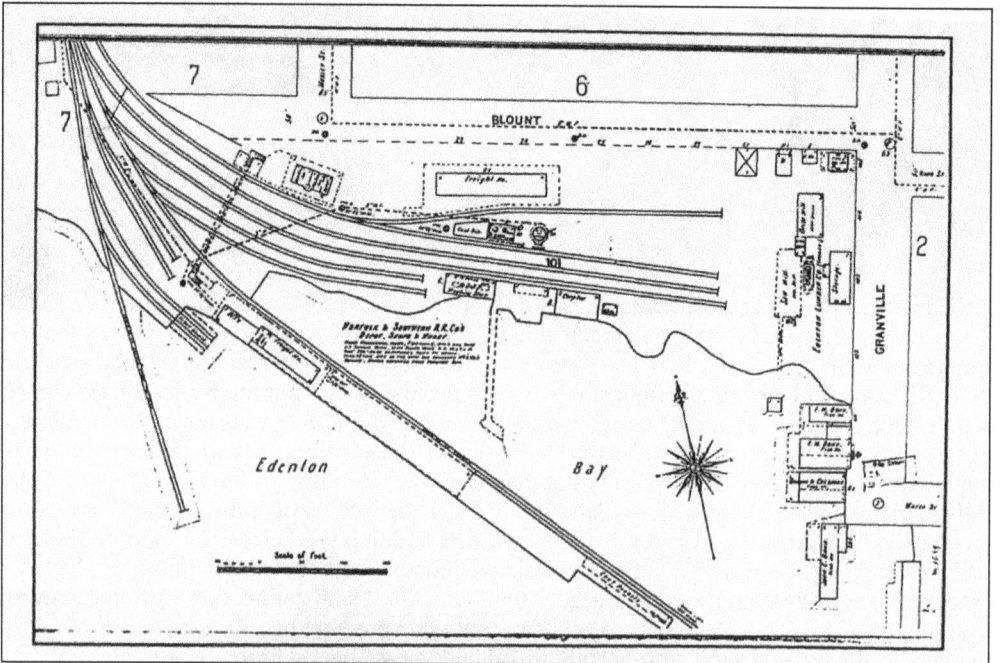

This 1904 Sanborn map shows the N&SRR waterfront complex along Blount Street in Edenton. (Courtesy of Sanborn Map Company.)

In 1907 the N&SRR took delivery of 7 new Baldwin B-5 4-4-0 engines. The engines had 18-inch-by-24-inch cylinders and were said to be the most powerful American-built engines at that time. A 1916 photo shows engine No. 54 on an Edenton sidetrack. (Courtesy of N&SRR.)

This N&SRR Mogul C-2 type 2-6-0, No. 104 engine was built by Baldwin in 1890. A 1908 photo shows a Baldwin engine standing on the Albemarle Sound trestle while it was still under construction. During construction there were several accidents. The south shore end of the trestle collapsed in 1909, and a Baldwin engine with two cars were lost—as was the engineer's life. The trestle was reconstructed and completed in 1910. (Courtesy of N&SRR.)

160 FT. STEEL DRAW ON BRIDGE ALBEMARLE SOUND, EDENTON, N.C. 559

In 1911 the Albemarle Sound trestle had two channel spans—a draw span over a 10-foot deep channel near the Edenton shore and a 152-foot-long Scherzer rolling lift-type steel draw span over a deeper channel near the middle. These lifts "required the services of two draw tenders 24 hours a day," said retired N&SRR employee and historian Bill Sellers. (Courtesy of HESHS.)

tor Car Crossing N. S. R. R. Bridge, Albemarle Sound; Length of Bridge, Five and Seven-tenths Miles, Edenton, N. C.

This was N&SRR motor bus No. 90 crossing the Albemarle Sound on the rail trestle in 1914. "These gas-powered motor buses were manufactured by McKean Co. of Omaha, Nebraska. They operated only in North Carolina. However, it did not prove economically feasible, and in 1923 they were equipped with electric motors and operated in Virginia Beach as a trolley until 1928," relates Bill Sellers. (Courtesy of Vernon Austin.)

A one-way steam engine excursion for rail fans crossed the Albemarle Sound railroad trestle from Edenton to Mackey's Ferry in August 1974 on its way to Raleigh. "This was the last steam locomotive to cross over that bridge before it was dismantled in 1987," said Bill Sellers, a native of Wilson, North Carolina. "This trip was sponsored by the Old Dominion Chapter of the National Railway Historical Society based in Richmond, Virginia." (Courtesy of Bill Sellers.)

Around 1950 the N&SRR made the switch from fossil fuel engines to the less pollutant and more efficient diesel engines. Here was Engine 702 heading south from Edenton. The Edenton Peanut factory can be seen in the background. Railroad fan Bill Sellers says "I still miss the majestic, hissing and puffing, steam engines that roamed our landscape for some 200 years." (Courtesy of PSML.)

On a hot and humid June 28, 1916, many Edenton families came to the train station. They brought umbrellas to block the sun. They waved and cheered good-bye to their North Carolina Regiment Company "T" sons as they loaded the N&SRR passenger and mail cars for the trip west to train near the Mexican border. (Courtesy of Corrine Thorud.)

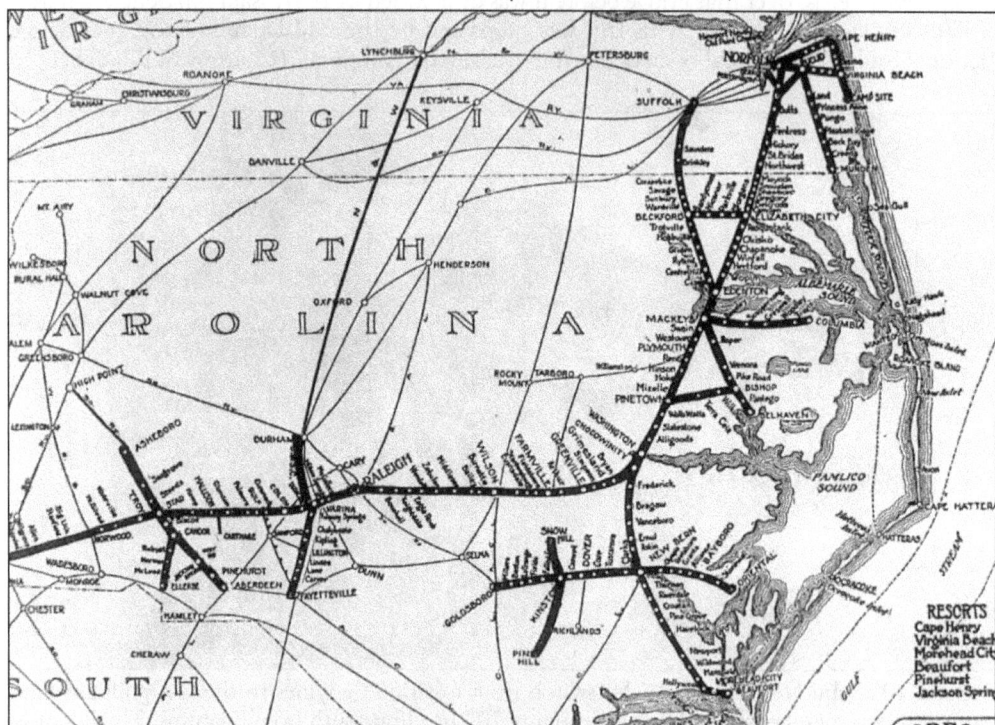

This 1920 map shows a portion of the 949 miles of track laid by the N&SRR from Norfolk, Virginia to Charlotte, North Carolina, and eastward to Beaufort, North Carolina. (Courtesy of N&SRR.)

Three

STEAMBOATS AND
THE RAILROAD SHIP

Although rail service ended at Edenton's water's edge in 1881, the steamboats of the Albemarle Navigation Co. filled the transportation void, offering service across the Albemarle Sound and up the Chowan River. The Old Dominion Steamship Line offered passage from Edenton and Elizabeth City to Norfolk and New Bern. In 1892 the N&SRR entered into a five-year lease agreement with Old Dominion. On the Pamlico River their *Haven Belle* carried passengers from Belhaven and Washington to Bayboro and Aurora. The *Norman L. Wagner* carried freight and passengers from Edenton to points south of the Albemarle Sound. The N&SRR purchased the *Plymouth* from the Roanoke, Norfolk, and Baltimore Steamship Co. and sailed her between Edenton and Plymouth. They also bought the former Baltimore and Ohio Railroad side-paddle train ferry, the *John W. Garrett*. By 1892 the N&SRR was operating a train ferry across the Albemarle Sound. This service continued until 1910, when their trestle was completed. The Dismal Swamp Canal connected Norfolk with the Albemarle Sound and was officially opened in 1829; it had five locks to control water depth. Eastern North Carolina steamers used this canal to transport commerce to northern markets. This scene portrays boats passing the Lake Drummond Hotel; the lake was named in honor of William Drummond, the first Governor of Albemarle County under the Lords Proprietors (1663–1667). Regarding the prospects of commerce, Hugh Williamston of Edenton wrote to George Washington in 1784, "I have long been satisfied of the practicability of opening communication between the waters which empty in Albermarle Sound thro' Drummond's Pond and the Waters of Elizabeth or Nansemond Rivers." By 1784 the Dismal Swamp Canal Company had been created. (Courtesy of MMNV.)

The *John W. Garrett*, under the command of Capt. Samuel Ferebee Williams (1849–1923), carried rail cars across the Albemarle Sound. This crossing usually lasted one hour and forty-five minutes. (Courtesy of N&SRR.)

The *John W. Garrett* was docking at Mackey's Ferry slip in 1908. In high winds, docking this 750-foot carrier could be a hair-raising experience for both passengers and boat crew. (Courtesy of N&SRR.)

This N&SRR depot at Mackey's Ferry, built in 1890, was a very important junction prior to 1910 while the railroad trestle across the Albemarle Sound was being completed. The *John W. Garrett* unloaded here, and the train cars were attached to a steam engine. There were three sets of track. One went southeast to Roper, Creswell, and Columbia. A second went south to Belhaven, and a third went west to Plymouth. (Courtesy of N&SRR.)

The N&SRR purchased the steamer *Plymouth* in 1887. The *Plymouth* was used as a passenger ferry between Edenton and Plymouth on the Roanoke River until 1910 when through railroad service began between those two towns. In 1908 Towers and Kenton Inc. of Baltimore, Maryland, purchased the *Plymouth* and in 1913 she was dismantled. (Courtesy of HESHS.)

The Suffolk & Carolina Railroad steamer *Edenton* (1871–1929) was in her homeport in 1906. This ship was originally the side-paddle *Bristol*, built by Woolston & Van Dusen of Philadelphia. It was converted to a screw steamer in 1905 and sold to the Albemarle Steam Navigation Company around 1909. (Courtesy of N&SRR.)

"The Albemarle Steam Navigation Company, was based in Edenton as one of the marine operations of the Norfolk Southern Railroad," said historian Bill Sellers. The ASN Company dates back to 1840 and furnished boats for the Confederate Navy during the Civil War. After the war "they operated up the Roanoke River as far as Halifax, and up the Chowan and the Meherrin Rivers all the way to Franklin Virginia," said Sellers. Shown above is the side-paddle steamer *Nanticoke*, which was built in 1875 as the *Chowan*. The *Chowan* was sold and renamed around 1880 and operated in the Baltimore Eastern Shore Service until she was returned to Chowan River service out of Edenton in 1903. (Courtesy of N&SRR.)

The passenger steamer *Norman L. Wagner* (c. 1882) was built in Buffalo, New York, for the John L. Roper Lumber Company of Norfolk. The N&SRR acquired her in 1891. The *Wagner*, shown moored at the N&SRR service dock in Edenton in 1906, carried passengers and freight to points south of the Albemarle Sound. (Courtesy of N&SRR.)

The *Haven Belle* was a grand steamer with fine accommodations. She was built of iron construction in Philadelphia in 1885 for the John L. Roper Company. The *Haven Belle* operated from Belhaven. She sailed down the Pungo River, across the Pamlico River, up the Bay River to Bayboro, or up South Creek to Aurora. The *Haven Belle* also went up the Pamlico River to Washington. In 1929 the *Haven Belle* was sold to Capt. B.G. Willis of who sailed her out of Edenton until 1933. She was then converted to an oil tanker that operated out of Norfolk into the 1970s. (Courtesy of HESHS.)

The U.S. Revenue Cutter *Pamlico* (*c.* 1897) collected shipping taxes on imports from West Indies ships until 1942 when she was refitted as a World War II mine sweeper. The Pamlico visited all of the major ports of Eastern North Carolina. Her homeport, however, was New Bern. (Courtesy of Oden's Store.)

In 1857 David Hunter Strother, under the pen name of Porte Crayon, sketched the side-wheel steamboat *Stag* on her way to Edenton from Plymouth, a run of 21 miles. The *Stag* made a daily run between these towns in two hours and five minutes each way, and was large enough to carry several horse-and-carriage rigs. (Courtesy of Strother File.)

Four

HISTORIC DOWNTOWN EDENTOWN

Revolutionary War cannons mounted at the foot of the Courthouse Green have stood guard since 1928. These cannons were part of a shipment of 45 for distribution to various ports for coastal defense in 1778. Payment problems from a poor tobacco crop that year kept 25 cannons from ever being delivered. In this scene cannons frame the Barker-Moore House, which was moved from 209 South Broad Street to 505 South Broad Street in 1952. The Barker House was renovated in 1968 and used as the Edenton Visitor Center. This was the home of Penelope Barker, the reputed leader of the Edenton Tea Party Resolves of October 25, 1774. This protest took place as a result of the Boston Tea Party in December 1773. (Courtesy of HESHS.)

Main Street storefronts were stylishly ornate in the 1890s. This aerial view was taken from the catwalk of the 60-foot water tower located on the south end of Water Street, just west of Main Street. It shows the east side of the "Cheapside" block. The building with the double awning and high pediment gable was the Josephine N. Leary building. Ms. Leary, born a slave, was a successful black businesswoman. She and her husband, Sweety Leary, were both barbers. However, she used the Leary building only as a rental property. The cross street was King Street, and the three-story building with the three-window elevator tower was the Woodard Hotel. (Courtesy of Ann Perry.)

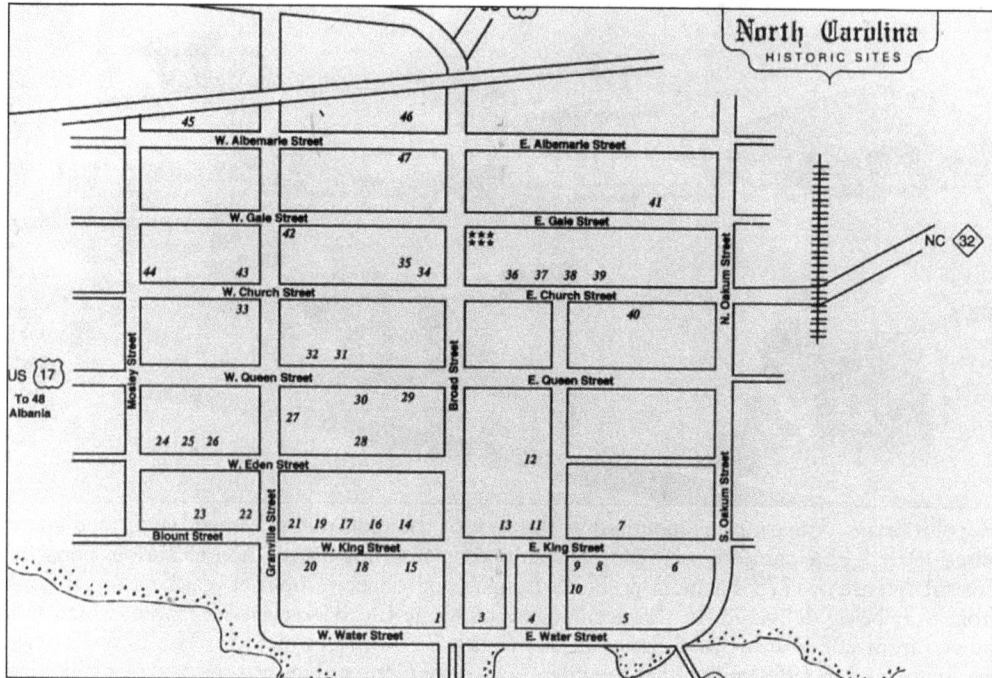

This map was reproduced from the "GUIDE BOOK, Historic Edenton and Chowan County," which also includes an index of 84 historic home sites. (Courtesy of HESHS.)

This 1900 picture of the Town Green, taken from Water Street, shows the 1767 Chowan County Courthouse (behind horse) on King Street. On the right is the Skinner-Bond House on Court Street, on the left is the Bay View hotel (dark building), and on the extreme left is the Homestead (*c.* 1773) with its Queen Anne addition (*c.* 1895). This addition was removed in 1956. (Courtesy of HESHS.)

This picture shows the town pump on the corner of Broad and West King Streets in 1900. From left to right are the Cupola House (*c.* 1758), the Edmund Hoskins Store (*c.* 1802) at 104 West King Street, and the Dr. William J. Leary Sr. building (*c.* 1872). The Leary building featured a flamboyantly shaped parapet gable with an oculus window. (Courtesy of HESHS.)

The Chowan County Courthouse (c. 1767) is located at 117 East King Street, seen here in 1900. This magnificent courthouse is considered by many to be the finest Georgian courthouse in the South, and is the oldest government building in North Carolina. The cupola was added in the 1770s. This building consists of a central courtroom with a large semicircular apse on the first floor flanked by adjoining offices. The handsome courtroom focuses on the elevated bar containing the chief justice's tall pediment chair. The exterior is made of Flemish-bond brick. The designer is thought to be John Hawkes of New Bern. (Courtesy of HESHS.)

The Courthouse Green is a rectangular plot which overlooks Edenton Bay at the foot of East Water Street and extends north to East King Street. This land has been public property since 1712. It was used as a drill field during the Revolution. The two diagonal paths were added in 1900. These paths crossed in the center at a raised pool, which contained an ornate cast-iron Victorian fountain. In 1904 a memorial to the county's Confederate dead was erected at the northern end. The fountain and Confederate monument were removed in 1961, and the green was terraced. The U.S. Congress erected the Joseph Hewes Memorial—one of the signers of the Declaration of Independence—in his honor at the south end of the Green in 1932. The Skinner-Bond House is seen on the left in this 1910 photo. (Courtesy of HESHS.)

The Edenton Masonic Lodge was located upstairs in the Chowan County Courthouse in the early 1900s, and is seen here in a 1929 postcard. The "throne" chair in the center was built and signed by craftsman Buck Trout, by commission of England's Queen Charlotte prior to the Revolution. In 1980, the Colonial Williamsburg Foundation purchased this chair from the Masonic Lodge for the sum of $212,500, and agreed to have their craftsmen make a replica to replace the original. The original chair is now on display at the De Witt Decorative Arts Museum in Norfolk, Virginia. (Courtesy of Ann Perry.)

This is a 1950s interior view of the Chowan County Courthouse. (Courtesy of NCSDA.)

Main Street, looking South,
Edenton, N. C.

This is a postcard view of the east side of Main Street (Broad) looking south around 1915. The building fronts had all been changed by then. (Courtesy of Ann Perry.)

By the 1920s gas street lamps had been installed on Main Street. This postcard view shows both sides of Main Street (Broad) looking south. The building on the left was the Woodard Hotel. Opposite on the right side was the two-story Citizen Bank building. The water tower, from which the aerial view on page 32 was taken, was located near Water Street approximately where the police station stands in the year 2001. (Courtesy of Ann Perry.)

This photo of Main (now Broad) Street looking north was taken around 1907 and shows the east side of the 300 block that had been rebuilt in the late 1890s. (Courtesy of HESHS.)

Business Section, Main Street, Edenton, N. C.

The entire business district was rebuilt after much of it was destroyed by fire in 1893. The Dixon Building (325–327), first on the right, was remodeled in 1895, as were the adjoining A.T. Bush (315) and the James Woolard Sr. buildings. (Courtesy of Ann Perry.)

The Cupola House (1758), seen on a 1920s postcard, was built for Francis Corbin at 408 South Broad Street. This large two-and-a-half story home is sheltered by a gable roof with a facade gable. The bell-shaped, octagonal cupola, which rises to a ball finial, provides a spectacular view of Edenton Bay. In 1918 the Cupola House Association was formed to save this building. The association altered the interior for use as a library, and in 1967 restored and furnished the house as a museum of the pre-Revolutionary period. (Courtesy of HESHS.)

The Wooten Store (c. 1900) had cast-iron details (since removed). Mr. Frank Wooten is seen in the center. As early as 1860 there were four ready-made clothing and tailoring shops and two milliners located in downtown Edenton. (Courtesy of SPML.)

This Neo-Classical Revival–style building (c. 1911) was Edenton's second bank, located at 400 South Broad Street and seen in a 1929 postcard. The United States Post Office building was constructed as an attachment to the south side of the bank in 1920. The bank's first president, Julien Wood, served for some 30 years. This bank merged with Peoples Bank and Trust in the late 1950s. A larger bank building was erected elsewhere in 1970–71. In 1986 this building was donated to the town, and renovated for use as municipal offices. (Courtesy of Ann Perry.)

The Twentieth Century Barber Shop is seen in the 1930s. It was located on the west side of Broad Street South in the old Edenton Savings and Loan Company building—occupied by BB&T in the year 2001. The man sitting on the left was Justice of the Peace Brat Cobb. In the first chair on the right was Roy Spry, with barber Snowden Mills. In the second chair was Joe Privott, with barber Raymond Mansfield. The third chair customer is unidentified, but barber Ernest White was attending him. The fourth chair customer, also unidentified, was being groomed by barber Jerry Twiddy. (Courtesy of J.A. Mitchener III and Dollie Mansfield.)

39

The Edenton City Hall and Fire Department was located on Broad Street between the Cupola House and the U.S. Post Office from about 1920 to 1966, when a new station was built. It is seen here in 1961. "The firemen slept upstairs," said former Fire Chief Lynn Perry. (Photo by Fred Habit Jr.; courtesy of EFD.)

Shown here in 1966 is the Edenton Fire Department crew with an old hose reel cart from the 1904–1923 era of fire fighting. From left to right are Bill Stallings, Allen Swanner, Jerry Peele, Lowell Gieseke, Steve Biggs, Phil Tant, Waverly Westbrook, Junius Britton, and William Crummey. (Courtesy of EFD.)

40

By 1930 the Edenton Fire Department had acquired two fine fire trucks. On the left, standing on the running board of the newly acquired 1929 American La France, was Fire Chief Richard Hall, and Tom Glavine was at the wheel. On the right, Al Owens was behind the wheel of EFD No. 1, a 1923 Reo. Chief Hall was the first salaried fire chief. Garf Swanner bought the American La France at a later date. (Courtesy of EFD.)

In 1966 the fire department crew posed for the opening of their new fire station on the corner of North Broad and Park Streets. From left to right are Fire Chief W.J. Yates, Thomas Goodman, Bertram Byrum, Walter "Monk" Mills, and Lynn Perry. (Courtesy of CCH.)

The Woodard Building at 311–313 South Broad Street was erected in 1885, seen here in 1910. This Victorian-style structure had an interesting seven-bay facade embellished with a bracketed cornice, paneled frieze, and boxed window hoods. The storefronts were identical and flanked with a central door leading to the second floor. James A. Wollard, Sr. operated a general mercantile and dry goods store from 1867 until his death in 1888. His son James A. Wollard Jr. (1866–1938) inherited the store and ran it until he died. In 1944 Edward Habit (1888–1952) bought 313, and ran a pool hall there during the 1940s. (Courtesy of HESHS.)

The Byrum Brothers Hardware store was located at 314 South Broad Street in 1919. This unit was built in 1914 by Branning Manufacturing Company and was purchased by George P. Byrum (1870–1952) and Thomas Campbell Byrum (1892–1968), who are seen in this 1919 picture. This business remained Byrum Brothers Hardware until 1946 when George A. Byrum incorporated as Byrum Hardware. In 1951 G.A. Byrum purchased store unit 316 in 1951 and store unit 312 in the 1970s. (Courtesy of George A. Byrum)

Mitchener's Pharmacy at 301 South Broad Street, seen here in 1999, has a valuable link to the past—a National Cash Register Company register from 1916. "The highest sale it can record is $69.99," said owner John A. Mitchener III. "In 1916, that amount was plenty. My grandfather, John A. Doc Mitchener Sr, didn't sell that much in a day, what with most items selling for a nickel or a dime," said John. After 83 years of use John retired his beautiful relic. The old register is now a novelty that draws much attention. Mitchener's Drug Store now uses an "idiot electronic register," says John, because "clerks are not required to think on their feet and keep math in their head." (Courtesy of J.A. Mitchener III.)

The John A. Mitchener Sr. (1880–1956) and Julius Craig Leary (1870–1938) Drug Store was built at 301 East Queen Street in 1920. Their store carried a full line of drugs and soda fountain items, but the store did not have a pharmacy. Julius Leary and his wife, Eulalia Hobbs Leary, resided upstairs. Ownership of the store remained in the Mitchener family until 1961. (Courtesy of HESHS.)

The interior of Mitchener's Pharmacy has changed considerably since this 1930s picture was taken. The polished tiled floor and decorative molded, metal ceiling have been covered over. The Frigidaire soda fountain is gone. Standing from left to right are Jacob Muth; John A. Mitchener Sr. (1875–1956), owner; Lewis Francis; M.A. "Gus" Hughes (1903–1983), assistant pharmacist; unidentified; Hubert Elliott; and Sheriff E.S. Norman. (Courtesy of J.A. Mitchener III; Photo by Janie M. Harrell.)

This was the artistic storefront of Mitchener's Pharmacy located at 301 South Broad Street in 1930. Notice the tile entry and floor and the back lite display cabinets with mirrors on the rear wall. (Courtesy of J.A. Mitchener.)

Attorney J.H. McMullan Jr. was mayor of Edenton in 1932. McMullan was one of the original directors of the Edenton Peanut Company in 1909. (Courtesy of HESHS.)

This was the Leary Brothers Storage Company in 1933. R. West Leary and his brother J. Clarence Leary were grain dealers and commission buyers of produce, peanuts, cotton, and seed. R. West Leary lived at 108 Virginia Road with his wife, Hazel Johnson Leary. His brother J. Clarence Leary (1896–1983) and his wife, Lillian Webb Leary (1902–1981), lived at 219 Queen Street in a brick gambrel-roof home they built in 1935. (Courtesy of CCAC.)

Dr. Charles H. Hines (1870–1921), a black physician, built Hines's Drug Store in 1910 at 316 South Broad Street. Dr. Hines married Julia Capehart (1886–1921), and they had a daughter Flossie Hines Modlin (1903–1984). Dr. Hines also built one-story rental homes at 400, 402, and 404 North Granville Street before 1920. These houses were of the "shotgun" form—where the rooms were located behind one another—a style that evolved in the West Indies. In front of the store, believed to be from left to right, are Alexander Paxton, Dr. Charles Hines, Dr. O.L. Holley, and unidentified. (Courtesy of Ann Perry.)

This interior view of Dr. Hines's Drug Store in the 1920s shows the beautiful wood cabinetry, the marble soda fountain, and the stenciled metal ceiling. The men, believed to be from left to right, are Alexander Paxton, Dr. O.L. Holley, Dr. Charles H. Hines, and unidentified. The meat market of Cecil B. Byrum occupied this store in the 1930s; it was later the Harrell and Leary Hardware Store. (Courtesy of Ann Perry.)

In 1910 Edenton had four fire stations. Three were white and one was black. The one pictured is believed to be the black fire station located at 102 North Broad Street. These four companies were consolidated into one company that occupied Kramer's Garage at 113 West Water Street in 1927. In 2001, this old garage is a restaurant called Kramer's Garage Bistro by the Bay. (Courtesy of PSML.)

Pictured in the mid-1960s are members of the John R. Page Masonic Lodge on Oakum Street. Seen from left to right are Marshall Jordon, Norfleet Bond, Penrose Rogers, Dr. O.L. Holly, Walter Wright, William Collins, Sim Collins Sr., Willie White, William Reeves, Oliver Carter, unidentified, and Bubba Wright. (Courtesy of Vernon Austin.)

The Woodard Hotel was located at 215–217 South Broad Street prior to 1874. This hotel had two separate hip-roofed blocks with a double-tier porch that spanned an 80-foot facade. In 1893, proprietor John L. Rogerson advertised that the "old and established hotel still offers first-class accommodations to the traveling public." Behind the porch awning was Ward's Shoe Shop, which was run by Julian and Lela Ward. In the middle was Ernest Ward's Barber Shop. The Woodard operated until the 1930s and was demolished in the late 1940s. (Courtesy of J.A. Mitchener III and Bob Pratt.)

The Bayview Hotel was located at 109 East King Street, and is seen here in the early 1900s. It was reconstructed as the three-story, brick Hinton Hotel in 1925. The first Bay View Hotel was built in 1885, and part of it was used as the post office in 1893. (Courtesy of HESHS.)

A large crowd gathered downtown near the bus station to watch the start of the November 1932 Peanut Festival. The highlight of the festival was the peanut-rolling contest held in the middle of South Broad Street. Mayor J.H. McMullan fires the starting gun, and with their nose guards to the ground, contestants push peanuts toward the finish line. (Courtesy of HESHS.)

These fine police officers had a staff picture taken in 1968. From left to right are the following: (front row) Sgt. Harold J. Lupton, Chief James Griffin, and William Clemmens; (middle row) Melvin Griffin, Wayne Mizelle, and Harvey Williams; (back row) John Parrish, Ray Griffin, and Willie Satterfield. (Courtesy of Ann Perry.)

49

The 1979 Bank of North Carolina Board of Directors, from left to right, are George Alma Byrum, Alton Elmore, West Leary, John Mitchener, Richard Hardin, Jack Habit, Albin Evans, Spec Jones, and West Byrum. (Courtesy of G.A. Byrum.)

Undertaker Louis F. Zeigler was a great admirer of the Studebaker Company (c. 1852). In 1917 Zeigler contracted for a Studebaker one-half-ton chassis and a J. Paul Bateman hearse body from local car dealer J.H. McMullen Jr. for the sum of $1,895. Pictured here in 1918, alongside his brand new Studebaker Hearse, was his son Haywood Sawyer Ziegler (1896–1969), who at age 21 was working for his father. Zeigler's wife, Fannie Keeter Ziegler (1900–1980), is believed to have been the first North Carolina woman to obtain a funeral director's license. In later years a grandson, Haywood Sawyer Ziegler Jr. (1923–1975), ran the business until it closed in the 1970s. (Courtesy of Evelyn Powell.)

Five

EDENTON NEIGHBORS

This 1915 picture of East Water Street shows (to the left) the old Chowan County Courthouse on East King Street, with the Civil War Monument directly in front. The Julian Wood home is on the right, followed by the Dr. William J. Leary Sr. house (which came to be known as the ghost house) and the James Holmes house. "Dr. Leary's son James really was a recluse," said lifetime resident Anne Rowe. (Courtesy of HESHS.)

On October 25, 1774, Penelope Padgett Hodgeson Craven Barker (1728–1796), the wife of attorney and colonial agent Thomas Barker, gathered a group of prominent women in Elizabeth King's Court Street home. This group of women signed a letter known as the Edenton Tea Party Resolves, protesting the passage of the British Tea Act of 1773, which was directly responsible for the Boston Tea Party. The Tea Party Resolves stated that the British House of Parliament was taxing Americans without representation. This letter appeared several weeks later in the *Virginia Gazette* in Williamsburg. (Courtesy of HESHS.)

This house, seen in 1915, was built in 1773 as a two-story, gable-front section on the east end of four building lots owned by silversmith Joseph Whedbee. Whedbee sold his home to James and Hannah Iredell in 1778. James Iredell Sr. (1751–1799) was a justice of the first United States Supreme Court. His widow made a small addition to the house in 1799, and his son added the main portion of the house in 1827. The Iredell House has been restored and furnished as a museum representing the 1775–1825 period by the North Carolina State Division of Archives. (Courtesy of Oden Store.)

The famous Edenton Teapot was made in 1910 to commemorate the Edenton Tea Party of October 25, 1774. This was the earliest known political action by women in the American colonies. The teapot was cast in brass by former Connecticut brass foundry craftsman Frank Baldwin (1854–1933) for Frank Wood (1858–1921) and his wife, Rebecca Anderson (Collins) Wood (1864–1921), the owners of Holmstead in 1881. The teapot was later mounted on top of a Revolutionary War cannon and now stands next to the iron fence of Homestead at 101 Water Street. (Courtesy of HESHS.)

John and Lydia Bonner Blount built Beverly Hall in 1810. This great brick home is located at 114 West King Street. John Blount had a private bank within his home, which became a branch of the State Bank of North Carolina. SBNC purchased Blount's "Brick Dwelling and Banking House" in 1816. This 1910 scene show the lovely garden and fountain of Beverly Hall. (Courtesy of HESHS.)

Dr. Richard Dillard Jr. (1857–1928) is seen dining in his Beverly Hall home in 1897. Dillard, a graduate of Jefferson Medical College in Philadelphia in 1879, was an avid gardener and botanist and a contributor to *House and Garden* magazine. He developed the "Rose Walk" and "Italian Garden" on the Beverly Hall estate. Dillard was also a knowledgeable local historian and served on the North Carolina Historical Commission. (Courtesy of HESHS.)

Wessington House is located at 120 West King Street. This 1850 mansion is one of the most prestigious antebellum homes in North Carolina. Representing a combination of French, Italianate, and Victorian forms, it was built for Dr. Thomas D. Warren (1817–1878) of Virginia. Warren married Penelope Johnston Dawson Skinner (1818–1841) in 1840. In 1843 he married Margaret Lavinia Coffield (1827–1854). Union officers occupied the house in 1862. It became known as the Graham House in 1880, the W.B. Shepard Esq. home in 1886, and was inherited by John Washington Graham in 1969. It became known as Wessington (the English equivalent of "Washington") in the 1930s, because of the Graham connection to the George Washington family tree. Widow Anne Graham Rowe said, "this 1890 scene shows a weekend family get-together." (Courtesy of Anne Rowe.)

William Biddle Shepard Esq. (1799–1852) and his wife, Ann Daves Collins (1804–1848), were ancestors of Anne Rowe of Wessington. He was a state legislator from Pasquotank County; she was reared at Somerset Plantation in Washington County. (Courtesy of Anne Rowe.)

This 1916 picture shows, from left to right, Annie Shepard Graham (1880–1969) at age 36, William Alexander Graham (1905–1992) at age 11, and John Washington Graham (1908–1980) at age 8. (Courtesy of Anne Rowe.)

Corner Church and Granville Sts., Dr. McMullen's Residence, Edenton, N.C.

This antebellum home, located at 200 West Church Street, was originally built for merchant Alexander H. Bond (1831–?) and Sarah R. Simpson Bond (1834–1894) in 1860. In 1891 Dr. John Henry McMullan and his wife, Lina Tucker McMullan (1845–1914), acquired and enlarged this house to a center hall plan by adding a two-story, double-pile block on the west end. (Courtesy of HESHS.)

GRANVILLE STREET, LOOKING SOUTH TOWARDS ALBEMARLE SOUND, EDENTON, N.C.

Granville Street runs parallel to Broad Street and was named in honor of Lord Granville. Francis Corbin (?–1767) was Lord Granville's land agent. He administered Granville's vast land district from his office in the Cupola House from 1750 until 1759 when he lost Granville's favor. This land district encompassed an area north of a line roughly connecting Washington, Smithfield, and Asheville, and the entire Albemarle region. The Albemarle region was considered to be the most politically powerful portion of the colony. (Courtesy of SPML.)

57

Sitting at the reins in her family surry was Emma Hudgins Badham Gardner (1896–1988), the wife of Edenton banker William Henry Gardner (1895–1956). Emma posed their surry in front of the Chowan County Courthouse in 1909. On her right was their daughter Bessie Badam Leary, and in her lap was their daughter baby Helen. (Courtesy of HESHS.)

The Littlejohn–Byrum House (c. 1790) was built at 218 West Eden Street for William Littlejohn (1740–1817), the commissioner of the Port of Roanoke, and his wife, Sara Blount Littlejohn (1747–1808). Theoderick Benjamin Bland, who owned a fishery, and his wife, Althea L. Benbury Bland, purchased it in 1889. Thomas Campbell Byrum (1892–1968), who was a hardware merchant, and his wife, Lillian D. Forehand Byrum (1894–1968), retained the house until 1945 when their son Thomas Campbell Byrum Jr. (1922–1987) purchased it. It has remained in family ownership ever since. This 1900 photo shows the Bland sisters in front of their home. (Courtesy of CCAC.)

This 1902 portrait shows John B. Parker (1863–1936) and his wife, Betty Satterfield Parker (1866–1943), with baby Thomas Edward Parker. Parker ran Bennetts Grist Mill from 1915 until 1929. He opened a country store near Valhalla in 1930, which he and his wife ran until 1938. The lady with the apron was Betty Parker. The man by the Sinclair pump is unknown. (Courtesy of Shirley Toppin Kirby.)

The Toppin family of Edenton celebrated the 50th wedding anniversary of Jennie and Nolan Toppin in 1969. In front are Jennie Parker Toppin (1902–1986) and Noland Bunch Toppin (1900–1975). Behind them, from left to right, are (white shirt) Troy E. Toppin Sr., Garland Toppin, Wilbur N. Toppin, Lillie Toppin Beaman, Earl McCoy Toppin, Hazel Toppin Spruill, Maurice F. Toppin, Shirley Toppin Kirby, Haurice Ray Toppin, Guy Leroy Toppin, Durward Bunch Toppin, and Larry Eugene Toppin. (Courtesy of Shirley Toppin Kirby.)

This view of West Gale Street looking north was taken near the intersection of Granville Street. In the center is a young girl named Lina Pruden (1899–2000) at age 10. Lina married George Mack. The lady on the left (holding the dog) and the man directly behind her in the shadow of the tree are thought to be her parents, attorney James Norfleet Pruden (1873–1921) and Penelope McMullan Pruden (1877–1967). The Gale Street Baptist Church is on the right. (Courtesy of HESHS.)

Vernon Austin (born 1932) is surrounded by his family in 1960. On Vernon's left is Patsy Austin (born 1953), his wife Gladys B. (born 1935), and his son Randy K. (born 1950). Vernon and his wife Gladys have been in business together since 1957, operating a convenience store called La Dall Inc., located at 309 North Oakum Street in Edenton. (Courtesy of Vernon Austin.)

John "Doc" Agrippa Mitchener (1875–1956) and his wife, Bessie Mae Mitchener (1894–1947), came to Edenton in September 1898 and "Doc" worked in the W.J. Leary Drug Store. "Then Doc managed the Dr. Hoskins Drug Store from 1899 until 1906, when he opened his own store," said John A. Mitchener III. Doc built the present 301 South Broad Street store in 1914. In 1927 Doc added a town favorite, a Frigidaire soda fountain. This quickly became the favorite meeting place of Edenton teenagers. (Courtesy J.A. Mitchener III.)

William "Cap" Oscar Elliott Jr. (1897–1975) and his wife, Nora Rawlinson Elliott, lived at 102 Blount Street. "Cap" was the son of William Oscar Elliott Sr. and Addie Shannon Rouse Elliott, and was born at Pembroke Hall. His father was a merchant and an incorporator of the Edenton Cotton Mill in 1899 and the second bank of Edenton in 1911, and a shareholder in the Edenton Peanut Company in 1909 and the Edenton Ice and Cold Storage Co. in 1901. Cap was a master mechanic and a long-standing member of Unanimity Lodge in Edenton. (Courtesy of CCCH.)

The Powell family is seen at Strawberry Hill Plantation (c. 1785) around 1920. From left to right are Mary Jordan Powell (1864–1946) and her husband Allen Powell (1853–1931), Henry Powell (1863–1931), and Mary's sister Adelia Jordan (1867–1946). Henry Powell was a farmer and landowner who lived with his brother at Strawberry Hill until 1919 when he married Pennie Small (1886–1972). The newlywed couple renovated a house Henry had acquired in 1910 from Mrs. V.C. Moore at 206 North Broad Street. This house is still occupied by the Powell family in 2001. (Courtesy of Penny Powell Binns.)

On December 16, 1979, Ret. Lt. Commander Henry Allen Powell telephoned his daughter Penny at Peace College in Raleigh, and his son Bud at Mount Olive College and gave them an order to come home for the weekend. He had scheduled photographer Allen Asbell to take an outdoor family portrait. It rained that day, so here is the indoor portrait made by Asbell. From left to right are Henry Allen Powell at age 50, Evelyn Harrell Powell at age 47, Penny Powell Binns at age 20, and Henry Harrell "Bud" Powell at age 18. (Courtesy of Evelyn Powell.)

Three good friends pose in front of the James Leary house on Water Street. From left to right are Bessie Hoskins, Mary Williams, and Allie Gardner. (Courtesy of Corrine Thorud.)

The 2001 generation of the Elliott family are (left side standing) James Douglas Elliott Jr. (born 1947) and Emily Brenda Elliott (born 1975); below them are Carol Denise Evans Elliott (born 1952) and their son James Douglas Elliott III (born 1985). (Courtesy of Pansy Elliott.)

The Graham-Rowe family gathered in the hall of Wessington in 1997. From left to right are the following: (front row) Anne Rowe, Dorothy Graham (at age 84), and Emily Rowe; (back row) John Graham, Lonnie Sieck, Carol Sieck, Ellison Sieck, and Debbie Hallyburton. (Courtesy of Anne Rowe.)

On March 16, 1936, the North Carolina Legislature came to Edenton for the first time. This group of Edenton young ladies were going shopping at the John C. Bond Hardware Store at 305 South Broad Street. From left to right are Corrine Forehand, Virginia Moore, Elizabeth Morain, Anne Chappel, Emily Howard, and Estelle Markham. (Courtesy of Corrine Thorud.)

Six

HISTORIC CHURCHES

Located at 100 East Church Street, St. Paul's Episcopal Church has been called "an ideal in village churches." The parish was formed in 1701, and the building was started in 1736 and completed in 1774. It fell into a state of decay after the Revolution, then received extensive renovation from 1806 to 1809 under the direction of English architect William Nichols of New Bern. The only exterior change was the addition of the spire that stands above the bell tower. From 1848 to 1850 new chancel furnishings were installed. (Courtesy of HESHS)

In 1806 St. Paul's interior was completely renovated. Floor tile was replaced by wood and the galleries were reconstructed. The sanctuary level was raised and a new pulpit, reading desk, and pews were added. (Courtesy of HESHS.)

First Presbyterian Church of Edenton is located at 200 South Mosley Street; its congregation formed in 1909. The church purchased the Methodist Protestant church at 404 North Broad Street in 1918 and renamed it the Mitchener Memorial Church. In 1928 the name was changed back to First Presbyterian. The present church was built in 1945–46 and the first service was held on Easter Sunday in 1946. Jane Love is the current pastor. (Photo by Louis Van Camp.)

This Colonial Revival–style Baptist Church at 206 South Granville Street was Edenton's third Baptist church, and was designed by Charlotte architect J.M. McMichael. The central dome has an oculus window filled with vibrant colored glass that radiates colors throughout the sanctuary. This 1920 picture shows it under construction. In the background is the second Baptist church (c. 1895). One of the first ministers was Rev. Thomas Meredith (1795–1850), who was pastor from 1825 until 1835. The Rev. Christopher W. Bailey was rector from 1868 until 1871. Bailey said that Meredith brought North Carolina Baptists "into unity of faith and work. He set their standards, cast their mold of thinking, and fixed the purpose of the lives of hundreds of thousands who came after them." (Courtesy of Corrine Thorud.)

The men's Baptist Sunday School class "is known as the largest men's class anywhere around," said Corrine Thorud. This 1944 picture includes the following: Jim Daniels, John A. Curran, Lloyd E. Griffin (who taught the class for 61 years), M.A. Huges, Earl G. Harrell, Carey Bunch, Haywood Bunch, Cecil Byrum, Lyn Byrum, Rodney Byrum, O.E. Duncan, Leroy Dale, John M. Elliott, Louis Francis, W.P. Goodwin, Wallace Goodwin, John M. Harrell, Louis Harrell, Evie Haste, Gurney Hobbs, Guy C. Hobbs, Leroy Haskell, Clayton Hollowell, Bill Israel, A.E. Jenkins, Rodney Jones, Willie Lamb, Leon Leary, R. West Leary, Roy Leary, Tex Lindsay, James O. Manning, Raymond Mansfield, Clyde Mason, Jack Mooney, Lee Moore, C.Y. Parrish, Ralph Parrish, Maynard Perry, William S. Privott, Henry Rogerson, Charlie Small, John Lee Spruill, T.B. Smith, Ernest Stillman, George Twiddy, and Wilford Turner. E.L. Wells was Pastor from 1911 to 1946. (Courtesy of Corrine Thorud.)

Bishop John England organized the Catholic Community of Edenton in 1821. The integrated congregation consisted of some 30 parishioners. The present St. Anne's Catholic Church is on the corner of South Broad and West Albermarle Streets—a Romanesque Revival building designed by architect L.L. Long of Baltimore and built in 1858. The Rev. Charles J. Grogan was pastor. In 1937 a wing was added, and Fr. Edward Gross became the first resident pastor. Today, this parish serves 220 people from five counties. (Courtesy of St. Anne's Catholic Church)

The Pleasant Grove A.M.E Zion Church, located at 123 East Carteret Street, was formed in 1866. The original church was located in Soundside but was closed in 1942 when the Marine Corp Air Base opened. Members attended Union Grove A.M.E. Zion Church until the present building was completed in 1946. Rev. E.J. Hayes, an educator and teacher from Williamston, was pastor. In 1980 an organ was purchased and organist Bobby Backus "would go from organ to the piano and the choir grew bigger and better," said parishioner Vernon Austin. (Courtesy of Vernon Austin.)

This Methodist Protestant Church was located at 402 North Broad Street and was built in 1900 with bricks furnished by the Edenton brick works. This congregation was the northern counterpart of the Methodist Episcopal Church South. The membership declined by 1919 and the church was sold to a newly organized Presbyterian group. This church was razed in the 1950s. (Courtesy of HESHS.)

The original interior of the Edenton Methodist Protestant Church featured a large semi-circular apse on the east and a low, three-stage bell tower on the west. Wooden columns and a gallery supported the cove ceiling across the rear. This 1900 picture shows the re-worked Federal interior done by architect William Nichols of New Bern between 1806 and 1809. (Courtesy of HESHS.)

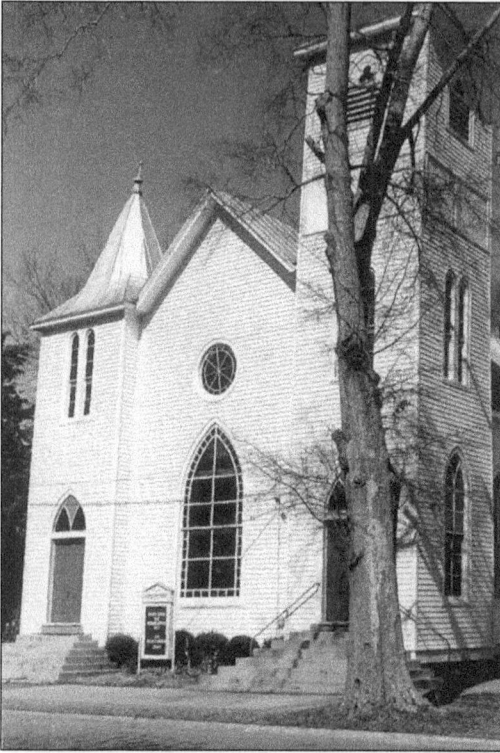

The Kadesh A.M.E. Zion Church was built in 1897 at 119 East Gale Street. This church was organized in 1866 by emancipated blacks to serve their religious, educational, and social needs. The name Kadesh was chosen because the Kadesh was the oasis in the wilderness where the Israelites encamped on their journey from Egypt to Canaan. This church is a strong example of a Victorian adaptation of the Gothic Revival style, and was built by member Hannibal Badham Sr. From 1908 to 1928 Kadesh members ran the Edenton Normal and Industrial College for black children in a large building behind the church. Edenton public schools then took over and taught black children grades one through seven until 1940 when the school was demolished. (Photo by Louis Van Camp.)

This Queen Anne–style A.M.E. Parsonage House was built in 1900, at 121 Gale Street, by Hannibal Badham Sr. (1845–1918). Badham was one of the leading black carpenters in Edenton during the late 19th and early 20th centuries. (Courtesy of CCAC.)

Rev. N.S. Parker is shown preaching at the Gale Street Baptist Church in 1948. Parker taught at St. John's Community School in the mid-1900s. (Courtesy of Vernon Austin.)

The Providence Baptist Church Choir performs a Christmas cantata under the direction of the Rev. W.C. Butts in 1965. From left to right are the following: (first row) Joseph Dixon, Mrs. Verta S. Pridge, Erma Copeland, Charlie Downing, Norfleet Bond, Mary H. Holly, Beatrice Jones, and Rev. W.C. Butts; (second row) Nora Bonner, Mrs. Slade, Roberta Banks, and Johnnie B. Sessons; (third row) Rosa B. Joyner, Flossie Hines, and Emma Slade; (fourth row) Erma Blount, Ethel Hudson, Lula Johnson, Mable Capehart, Barbara White, and Kathryn Sharpe Novella, and unidentified. (Courtesy of CCAC.)

The John R. Page Masonic Lodge (c. 1890) is located at 116 North Oakum Street. This lodge was originally known as the Pride of the South Odd Fellows Lodge. It is the only survivor of six fraternal halls erected by Edenton blacks between 1885 and 1927. The original directors were E.W. Whedbee, J. Willis, and J.E. Creecy. It was named in honor of John R. Page (1840–1881), a fine post–Civil War black carpenter. (Photo by Louis Van Camp.)

The Providence Baptist parish was formed in 1868 when emancipated blacks began forming separate congregations. It is located at 214 West Church Street. The congregation first met in an old school house on Freemason Street, but by the 1880s they had erected a frame building. The building shown was constructed in 1893. This church also operated a sectarian elementary school in a two-story home on the adjacent lot from about 1908 to 1926. A new church school was added in the rear of the existing building in 1955. (Photo by Louis Van Camp.)

The First Christian Church (c. 1916) is located on McMullan Avenue and was erected for the cotton mill workers. The congregation formed in 1924 and held their services at the courthouse. When this building became available the same year, they purchased it. Most of the present congregation lives in the old mill village. The white frame building in the background was erected as a Sunday School annex in 1949, but was converted into a social building in the mid-1970s. (Photo by Louis Van Camp.)

St. John the Evangelist Episcopal Church was founded in 1881 at 128 East Church Street. This church was rebuilt in 1887, and enlarged between 1910 and 1920. The interior of this Gothic Revival–style church is spanned by trusses that mimic a hammer-beam ceiling. The sanctuary centers on an exquisite chancel and rood screen. Behind the alter is a stained glass window dedicated to the memory of John R. Page (1840–1881), a leading post–Civil War black builder, and his wife Jane R. Page (1839–1903). The church "ran a school for grades one-through-eight black children from 1892 to 1902," said Rosa B. Joyner. (Courtesy of SPML.)

73

The Rocky Hock Baptist Church was founded in 1835 as the Church of Christ of Rocky Hock. Robert Felton gave the land, "to build on by consent," and Elder John B. Webb was the first pastor. The one-room frame building shown was built in 1858, and the congregation met there once a month. (Courtesy of Rocky Hock Church.)

Rocky Hock had around 750 members in 1996. (Courtesy of Rocky Hock Church)

The Rev. Bomar L. Raines conducted a Rocky Hock Baptist Church baptismal ceremony at Bass Landing on the Chowan River in 1957. Shown here from left to right are (front row) Joe Bass, Arlon Bunch, Carroll Tynch, Thomas Peele, unidentified, Roy Nixon, Ellis Tynch, and unidentified; (back row) Betty Lou Lane, Judy Haste, Reba Perry, unidentified, Jeanette Nixon, unidentified, Shelia Leary, and two unidentified. (Courtesy of Rocky Hock Church.)

These were the members of the 1965 Rocky Hock Choir. The choir director was Lloyd Wayne Evans. From left to right are the following: (front row) Janie Harrell, Kathryn Tynch, Etta Rea Bunch, Ruby Lee Bunch, Nancy Spivey, Mary Allred, and Lloyd Wayne Evans; (middle row) Robert Harrell, Jessie Goodwin, Lillie Saunders, Pearl Harrell, Dellie Bass, Irene Bunch, Bessie Harrell, Eunice Bunch, and Mary Perry; (top row) Charlie Peele, Thurman Alred, Sammy Byrum, Carroll Evans, Wallace Evans, and Jack Evans. Our "choir loves all the old standard hymns and does a Christmas Cantata every December. They also have other special musical presentations during other holiday seasons throughout the year," said the present-day choir director Jack Evans. (Courtesy of Jack Evans.)

These were the children of the 1943 Young Women's Association, which was sponsored by the Women's Missionary Union. Listed from left to right are the following: (bottom row) Louise Bunch, Marie Bunch, Lois Bryant, and Eloise Bunch; (second row) Lillian Privott, Grace Bunch, Mildred Harrell, and Juanita Harrell; (third row) Sallie Marie Harrell, Ruth Morris, Ruth Evans, and Ethel Harrell; (fourth row) Louvennia Morris, Edith Bunch, Loraine Bunch, Helen Evans, Celia Rae Nixon, and Hurley Winborne. (Courtesy of Rocky Hock Church.)

The white-frame, one-room Evans United Methodist Church is located on NC 32 North and Mavaton Road. The arched, stained glass window over the entrance reads "Evans M.E. Church/Founded 1826/ Rebuilt 1888/ Remodeled 1913." Zachariah Evans (1781–1857) from Hertford County, the founder, had been ordained a deacon by Bishop Hedding in Norfolk, Virginia, in 1836. This church has always served an interracial congregation and was used as the Faith Fellowship Baptist Church during much of the 1990s. Recently renovated, it is now being used as the Fellowship Worship Center. (Courtesy of SPML.)

Seven

EDENTON AND CHOWAN COUNTY SCHOOLS

The Edenton Academy, a private, white school, was chartered in 1770 by Joseph Blount, Joseph Hewes, George Blair, and Samuel Johnson. The first academy was built in 1891 by contractor J.W. Spruill on Court Street between East Church and East Queen Streets. In 1895 a new academy—shown c. 1905—was built on the same site and used as a public white school until Edenton Graded School was erected in 1916. The Academy had a central hall with two classrooms on either side. (Courtesy of HESHS.)

The Free School (*c.* 1851) was a one-story public school for white children located at 205 South Oakam Street. Pictured around 1895 was a class of mixed grade students. (Courtesy of HESHS.)

This is thought to be a 1905 class of the Academy. From left to right are the following: (first row) John ?, Delia ?, Gertrude Boff, unidentified, Julia Batson, Scott Privott, Lizia ?, Bertha ?, and Elmer Duib; (second row) Burt Layton, ? Jones, Buelah Griffin, Ella Holloman, Ida Forehand, Baker ?, Larry ?, and Phil Holley; (third row) Mary Layton, Mary Evans, Will Goodwin, Viola Elliott, Beth Elliott, Maggie Evans, Johnny Goodwin, and Georgie White; (fourth row) Miss Addis Watkins and Cassion Edd Griffith. (Courtesy of CCAC.)

Edenton High School—originally Edenton Graded School—was built in 1916 on the Court Street site of the old Edenton Academy between East King and Queen Streets. The flanking wings were added in 1926, and a large auditorium in the early 1930s. It remained the local high school until the 1950s when it became the Ernest A. Swain Elementary School; it was consolidated with D.F. Walker Elementary in 1985. In 1988, Winston-Salem developer DeWayne Anderson, in collaboration with Chowan County and the Historic Preservation Foundation of North Carolina, divided the classrooms into 38 apartments. The rear south side of this building now houses the Chowan Arts Council and a museum. (Courtesy of HESHS.)

The original Chowan High School, built in 1934, was located on Highway 32 N near Mavaton Road and consisted of grades one through eleven. Chowan High School was integrated in 1968, was changed to a middle school in 1989, and was torn down in 1991. A new middle school was then built on the same grounds. (Courtesy of Jack Evans.)

The John A. Holmes High School (*c.* 1950) is located on Woodard Street between East Freemason Street and Park Avenue. The trustees were Thomas Chears (chairman); William Bond; Walter A. Leggett; Joseph H. Congers; Philip S. McMullan; and John A. Holmes (secretary). The school consists of grades eight through twelve. The building architect was Frank W. Benton. (Photo by Louis Van Camp.)

The Edenton High School for Blacks was erected on the corner of North Oakum and School Streets, with assistance from the Rosenwald Fund, in 1932; it was destroyed by fire in 1972. In 1973, the D.F. Walker Elementary School was built on the same site. Pictured here in 2001, the school consists of grades one through five. (Photo by Louis Van Camp.)

John Albert Holmes (1890–1961) and his wife, Willie McDonald (Barrett) Holmes (1895–1954), came to Edenton from Raleigh in 1922. For the next 38 years Holmes served as school superintendent with such distinction that Edenton High School was renamed in his honor in 1950. (Courtesy of Ann Perry.)

The Rocky Hock congregation has always taken great pride in their adult Sunday School classes. The 1961 class included, from left to right, (front row) Nora Oliver, Bailey Miller, Effie Evans, and Myrtle Peele; (middle row) Ruth Harrell, Martha Nixon, Fannie Bunch, Bessie Boyce, Mary Harrell, Mary Nixon (teacher), Martha Peele, and Bertha Layton; (back row) Nora Forehand, Artie Bass, and Ada Byrum. (Courtesy of Hocky Rocky Church.)

The Black Edenton High School Faculty for 1948–49 was lead by Principal D.F. Walker, who served from 1932 until 1969. To his right is Miss L.M. Tillett, and on his left is B.C. Newsome. From left to right on the bottom row are T.I. Sharpe, J.A. Bennett, and Miss Ozetta Price. Edenton High was built under the Rosenwald Fund in 1932, and housed grades one through eleven until 1948. "In 1949, the curriculum changed to twelve grades. The class of 1949 was the first class to graduate under the new program," said retired teacher Mr. T.I. Sharpe. (Courtesy of Lula Jones.)

Mrs. M.M. Tillett's (on left) 1959 piano class included Randy Austin, Patsy Austin, Patrica Fayton, Joseph Tillett (her grandson), Emma Hathaway, Joseph Hathaway, Evette Tillett (her granddaughter), Ewing Sesson, Thersea Hathaway, Francis Hathaway, and Joanne Walton. (Courtesy of Vernon Austin.)

Members of the 1948–49 Edenton High School girls basketball team, from left to right, are (front row) Annie Johnson, Elizabeth Taylor, Lula Johnson, (sitting) Mildred Harris, Sawyer Holly, Julia Brown, and Thelma Simmons; (middle row) Linelle Small, Mary Roberts, Virginia Drew, and Martha Wood; (back row) Marion Paxton, Bessie Beasley, Jacqueline Coston, and Van Dora Murdough. (Courtesy of Lula Johnson.)

Chowan County resident Amelia Bond instructed the 1999 Lawrence Academy Tennis Team at 148 Avoca Farm Road, Mary Hill, North Carolina. From left to right are the following: (top row) Heather Parker, Katina Summerford, Emily Boehling, Melissa Perry, and Courtney Spear; (bottom row) Elizabeth Dixon, Lauren Greene, Jennifer Dickens, Erin Potaki, and Bri-Annna Mathews. (Courtesy of Amelia Bond.)

The graduating home economics class of Edenton High School for Blacks in 1941 included Lula Tillott, Margaret Blount, Odessa Privott, Francis Chandler, Arnetta Cox, Anne Newey, Dinah Robbins, Doris Blount, ? Rebell, Miss Sanford, Emma Jane Rogers, Emma Nichols, Emma Harris, Lessie Hathaway, Catherine Benbury, Mable Wills, Cora Lee Johnson, Marie Roberts, and Viola Roberts. The teacher was Miss Bias. (Courtesy of Vernon Austin.)

Edenton High School for Blacks was located at the south side entrance of the Rosenwald School, which was built in 1932 on North Oakam Street. This school burned down in 1972. The 1938 teachers were, from left to right, (front row) (torn ?), Flossie Hines, Mrs. Eunice Heritage, Emma Foreman, Butler Holley, and Fannie Badham; (middle row) (torn?), unidentified, Mrs. Wilson, and Principal D.F. Walker; (back row) Mrs. Percey Reeves, Mr. Alexander Blaine, Mrs. Charlton, and Mr. R.I. Kingsberry. (Courtesy of Vernon Austin.)

On November 2, 1927, Edenton High School was the first to use Hicks Field to play football—the land was a gift to the Town from Robert Hicks in 1723. Pictured on the back row are Coach Frank Suttenfield (left) and Manager Ercell Webb. The players include Raymond Everett, William Stokely, Paul Sexton, Carroll Goodwin, Guy Hobbs, Edward Cullipher, Joe Northcott, Rufus Bunch, Thomas Chears, Lesslie Morgan, Albert Cullipher, Joe Webb, Julius Wilder, James Boyce, Joe McNair, Meredith Jones, Carlton Mason, Lennie Bunch, Luther Bunch, Joseph Long, Fletcher Russell, and Thomas Satchwell. (Courtesy of SPML.)

Teacher Cleo G. Gardner's little "Sunbeams" of 1905 include from left to right (back row) Miles Chappell, Rodney Byrum, Thomas Alderman, Fred Bond, and Edgar Holmes; (second row down) Henry Privott, Grahm Hedrick, W.E. Bond, Clarence White, Harry Creecy, Julius Leary, and ? Lackland; (third row down) unidentified, unidentified, Iva Mae Dail, Margaret Nowell White, Julia Brinn, Myrtle Waff, Ila Leary, Jacqueline Chappell (Potter), Agnes Chappell, ? Lackland, unidentified, Mary Etheridge (Privott), Bertha Holmes, and Elizabeth Hollowell; (front row) Portia Alderman, Mary Hester Lewis, Agnes White (Harless), Virginia White, Louise Alderman, Evelyn Leary, Georgia Simpson, Elizabeth Bush, Fannie Lip, Dorethy White, Iona Wells, unidentified, Ruth Rea Holmes (Elliott), Virginia New, and Stella Holloman. (Courtesy of Corrine Thorud.)

The Rocky Hock Chowan Academy third-grade class visited a local flower farm in 1967. Standing tall, proud, and happy is teacher Mrs. Lena Jones. From left to right are the following: (back row) Monissa Hollowell, Vicki Chappell, and Penny Powell; (front row) Amanda Bunch, Arlese Monds, and Pam Berryman. (Courtesy of Evelyn Powell.)

Ms. Sara Wood's (center rear) class of 1930–31 are, from left to right, (first row) ? Turnstall, Anne Chappell, Marie Longdale, Murray Small, ? Shaw, and ? Eason; (second row) unidentified, J.L. Baker, Cathrine Reaves, unidentified, Pattie Garrett, Emma Alexander, Laura Dixon, Corinne Forehand, and Hazel Twiddy; (third row), Sammy Cates, Jimmy Hassell, Luther Parks, ? Byrum, Donald Ambrose, Robert Satterfield, three unidentified, Beulah Williams, and unidentified; (fourth row) unidentified, Elizabeth Street, Margaret Upton, unidentified, Meridith Jones, Dick Badham, Jimmy Davenport, Theodore Roberts, Wilbert Wheeler, and Madison Phillips. (Courtesy of Pansy A. Elliott.)

In 1925, the Edenton Swain Baseball Team included, from left to right, (top row) James Woolard White, Coach C.D. Stewart, and Gerald Owens; (second row down) William Stokley, Joe Campen, Skinner White, and Raymond Mansfield; (third row down) Joe Webb (in the arms of) Wilbert Russell, Ercell Webb, (girl) Boots Badham, Earl Goodwin, and William Privott. (Courtesy of Corrine Thorud.)

The 1928 *Tea Pot* editorial staff of Edenton High included, from left to right, (bottom row) Nell Nelson Powell, Ada Cozzens, Hazel Lane, Syble Haskett, Helen Russ, Ercell Webb, Ruth Thorson, and Margaret Hollowell; (top row) Thomas Chears and George Barrow. (Courtesy of SPML.)

The 1964 Chowan High School boys baseball team, from left to right, are as follows: (back row) Billy Lane, Fahey Byrum, Robert Bulls, Millard Joyner, Keith Rollins, Thomas Peele, Gene Harrell and Wayne Copeland (?); (front row) Joe Bass, Wyane Lane, Bobby Winborne, Arlyn Bunch, Billy Nixon, James Ward, and Jacob Jordan. (Courtesy of Pansy Elliott.)

The fifth-grade class of Edenton Swain Elementary School of 1959–1960 are, from left to right, (first row) two unidentified, Danny Hassell, Ann Jordan, Danny Jones, and unidentified; (second row) Fontaine Boutwell, Francis Bembridge, unidentified, Libby Baer, Jessie Cartwright, Iris Jean Bass, Ray Goodwin, Sylvia Jordan, and (against the back wall) teacher Ruth D. Bunch; (third row) Guy Williams, Tommy Robey, Johnny Dowd, Clara Blanchard, Linda Ashley, Brian Twiddy, and Gene Perry; (fourth row) Jimmy Rogerson, Anne Graham, unidentified, Gary Liverman, Mike Spruill, Tillie Cordon, and Cisco O'Neal. (Courtesy of Anne Rowe.)

The 1965 Edenton High football team was the top 2-A team in North Carolina. The defensive squad are, from left to right, (back row) Steve Davenport, Ronnie Harrell, Quinton Goodwin, Wesley Chesson, Buddy White, Mike Spruill, Tony Twiddy, and Frankie Katkaveck; (front row) Dwight Flanagan, Ikey Davis, Jim Elliott, and John Lavezzo. (Courtesy of Pansy Elliott)

The 1949–50 Edenton High School Glee Club members are, from left to right, as follows: (first row) Dorothy Henniger, Joyce Webb, Evelyn Harrell, Juanita Bennett, Gapie Daniels, Glenn Twiddy, Grace Hudson, Clara Dixon, Cecola Ward, Vera Boyce, Frances Bennett, Pearl Halsey, and Lucille Winslow; (second row) Doris Miller, Syble Cayton, Virginia Downing, Marge Dale Spry, Suzanne Speight, Betty Byrum, Jane Spry, Dorethy Baker, Jackie Langdale, Bessie Tynch, Frances Brown, Lillian Leary, and Peggy Williams; (third row) Mary Leggett Browning (teacher), Ann Harless, John Ward, Emmett Eason, Ralph Bennett, Stanford Spruill, Keith Emminizer, Johnny Owens, Carroll Copeland, Malcolm Eason, and Marjorie Thigpen; (fourth row) Charles Morgan, Donald Batton, John Jones. Charles Overman, Billy Bond, Ashton Morgan, Johnny Goodwin, Gary Martin, and unidentified. (Courtesy of Evelyn Powell.)

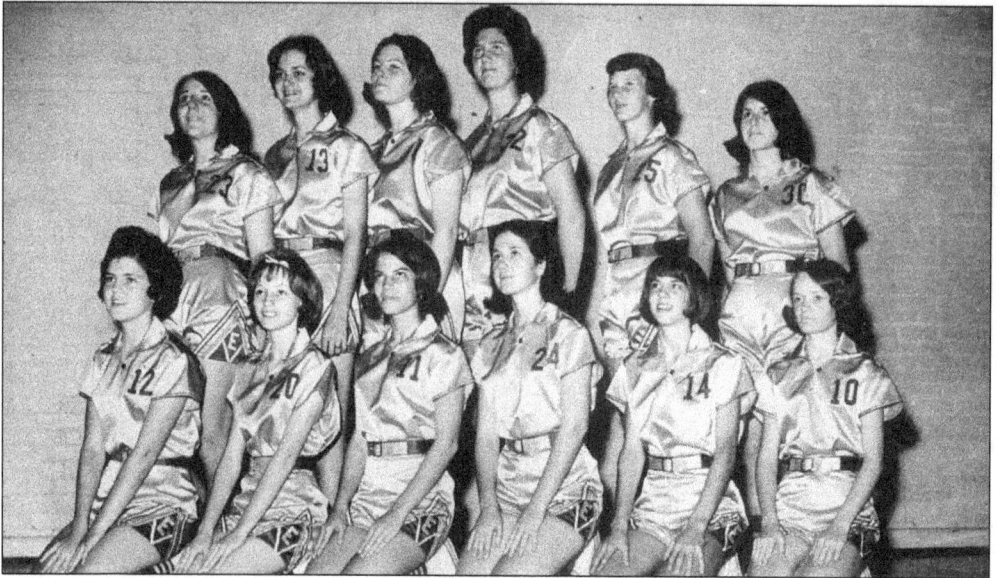

The 1966 John A. Holmes High School Acelets girls basketball team are, from left to right, (kneeling) Helen Pruden, Sandy Wynn, Sanfra Ange, Ann Castelloe, Rita Mayo, and Patricia Alexander; (standing) Judy Goodwin, Helen Jernigan, Becky Williford, Sue Powell, Beth Moore, and Anna Perry. (Courtesy of SPML.)

Eight

CHOWAN COUNTY

Cultivation of peanuts began in Chowan County in 1879 with 21 planted acres that yielded only 113 bushels. By 1889 this industry had expanded to 3,909 planted acres, and to 6,061 planted acres by 1909 when the Edenton Peanut Company was formed. The first officers were Thomas H. Shepard, president; H.G. "Hal" Woods, vice-president; and Thomas W. Warren, secretary and treasurer. The plant was located on East Church Street Extended and was serviced by a N&SRR side track that was formerly the main line of the Suffolk and Carolina Railroad. This line ran directly from Edenton to Suffolk, Virginia, where the main peanut processing plants were located. By 1927 this facility was milling over 1,500 bags of peanuts daily. The company was sold to the Birdsong Corporation of Suffolk in 1957 and closed the next year. (Courtesy of HESHS.)

The Edenton Cotton Mill, pictured here in 1915, was founded in August 1898 by several of the town's leading businessmen. Investors included planters Edward Wood Jr. and Fred A. White; banker Julien Wood; attorneys William D. Pruden, Haywood C. Privott, Edmund R. Conger, and C.S. Vann; merchant Abram T. Bush; undertaker Louis F. Ziegler; contractor Theo Ralph; and lumberman John W. Branning. (Courtesy of PNC.)

This 1958 photo shows the Edenton Cotton Mill twisting machines that were installed as part of a long-term plant modernization program completed in 1957. (Courtesy of PNC.)

Phillip McMullan, president and treasurer, managed the Edenton Cotton Mill. Dr. Frank Wood was vice-president, and Richard Elliot was secretary and assistant treasurer. The plant superintendent was C.A. Phillips until the mill closed in 1995. (Courtesy of PNC.)

This aerial view shows the Cotton Mill Village rental homes that were built adjacent to the mill in 1972. (Courtesy of PNC; photo Mike Williams, Aerial Dimensions.)

In November 1995, the Edenton Cotton Mill was closed after 97 years of operation. The corporate officers of Unifi Inc. of Greensboro deeded the mill and the 57 village houses to Preservation North Carolina. PNC made special arrangements for the mill employees to purchase or continue renting their homes. Mill Village children pass by on their way home from school. (Courtesy of PNC; photo by Gary Allen.)

Cotton, which the local farmers called "White Gold," was one of Chowan County's leading crops. Shown here around 1910 was a group of W.J. Webb farm workers in Yeopin picking cotton. On the right, the man in the white shirt is thought to have been W.J. Webb Sr., and next to him was foreman James Bonner. (Courtesy of CCAC.)

William Hutchings Winborne worked on the Martinique Plantation in northern Chowan County during the 1950s. Hutchings is pictured here "explaining the process of air drying tobacco to our children in 1955," said Mrs. Hurley Winborne. However, the children seem to have been more interested in eating watermelon than how their father air-dried his tobacco. (Courtesy of Mrs. Hurley Winborne.)

The Bandon Plantation was located some 12 miles north of Edenton. Edward Moseley was granted this acreage in 1711. Parson Daniel Earl, the rector of St. Paul's Episcopal Church in 1757, owned the first plantation house. The home pictured was built by Charles Johnson, Earl's son-in-law, around 1804. It burned down in 1963. Mr. and Mrs. Inglis Fletcher, pictured here, bought Bandon House in 1944, and Inglis Fletcher used Chowan County and Albemarle settings for many of her 12 history-based Carolina novels. (Courtesy of HESHS.)

Minna Towner Englis [Inglis?] Clark Fletcher (1879–1996) was born in Alton, Illinois. She married John George Fletcher on April 16, 1902. The couple were photographed in the living room of their Bandon Plantation House in 1944. Inglis once said that her twelve *Carolina Series* novels, which were published between 1942 and 1948, "were an attempt to illustrate the struggle of the common man and the 'gentle born' in their effort to establish a sound government in the wild." Inglis was active in the Iredell House restoration in 1948, and was one of the first nine recipients of the annual Cannon Cup award for outstanding work in the field of North Carolina historic preservation. (Courtesy of SPML.)

Athol (c. 1836) was an impressive Greek Revival–plantation house located some six miles east of Edenton. It was built by Joshua Skinner Jr. (1797–1852) and his wife, Elizabeth Blair Skinner (1802–1852). The couple lived there until their deaths in 1852. Julian Woods then occupied Athol. George D. Smith (1889–1951) and his wife, Sallie Louise Woolard Smith, worked the Athol farm for Julian Woods for several years before moving into Edenton. In 1943 the United States Marine Corps Air Station occupied most of the former Athol and Montpelier plantations, which were once among the county's most prosperous Albemarle Sound fisheries. (Courtesy of NCDAH.)

George C. Woods (1890–?), who lived in Deerfield, is seen in 1905 with "nanny" Amy Johnson (of Locust Grove) and childhood playmate Frank L. Williams of Greenfield. (Courtesy of HESHS.)

Richard Coffield (1853–?) was a Chowan County farmer. In 1900 he was a widower with two children—Richard Jr., born in 1885, and Annie, born in 1888. This picture was probably taken around 1895. (Courtesy of HESHS.)

Pre-Revolution Sycamore Plantation, Edenton, North Carolina

The Sycamore House (c. 1660) was located off of SR 1110 on a pre-revolution plantation owned by Thomas Norcom. The Norcom family occupied it until 1903. The floors, mantels, and paneling are all of the original woodwork. (Courtesy of NCDAH.)

These portraits of Dr. James Norcom (1778–1850) and Mrs. Marie Hornblow Norcom (1794–1868), by Joshua Reynolds, express the style of dress of the gentry in the early 1800s. Dr. William Norcom (1836–1881), the son of Dr. James Norcom, had his medical office at 105 East King Street. (Courtesy of NCDHA.)

Sandy Point Plantation was located on Sound Shore Road east of Edenton. Thomas Pollock, governor from 1712 to 1714 and again in 1722, and his wife, Esther, owned this fishery in the early 1720s. Thomas Luten inherited Sandy Point from widow Ester Pollock. Luten's daughter later married merchant Robert Hicks. In 1851 Sandy Point was owned by Richard Paxton (1819–1864) and his wife, Elizabeth Creecy Benbury Paxton (1821–1906), who told her sister that the house was "so much larger than any I have ever before lived in that I sometimes feel lost." This house remained in the Paxton family until 1925; it was acquired in 1948 by Frank Wood (1902–1963), a great-grandson of the Paxtons, and his wife, Martha Michael Wood (1899–1982). (Courtesy of HESHS.)

"Together at the home place," was written on the bottom of this print of the Edwin and Linda Byrum house in Rocky Hock. Their house was built in 1850. (Courtesy of CCAC.)

The Hayes Plantation house, named for Hayes Barton England, was built around 1815 by an African-American slave carpenter named Joe Welcome, who was owned by planter Josiah Collins Sr. (1735–1819) who came to the colonies in 1773. Brickmaker James Cunningham laid the brickwork. Hayes Plantation sits on a knoll overlooking Albemarle Sound. It was the home of North Carolina Governor Samuel Johnston (1787–1789), who later became the first U.S. Senator from North Carolina. His son James C. Johnston (1782–1865) resided here. Farmer Henry G. Wood owned Hayes Plantation in the early 1900s. (Courtesy of HESHS.)

The Mulberry Hill Plantation on Countryside (Road 114) was established by Capt. James Blount in 1684. By 1776 it belonged to his great-grandson, another James Blount and his wife, Anne Hall. Their son Clement Hall Blount built the house shown around 1810. He operated a fishery on the sound but was forced to sell in 1830. The Edward Wood family has owned Mulberry since 1865. This Federal-style house has a fan-shaped gable window and beautiful interior woodwork. The entrance portico is a 20th-century addition. (Courtesy of HESHS.)

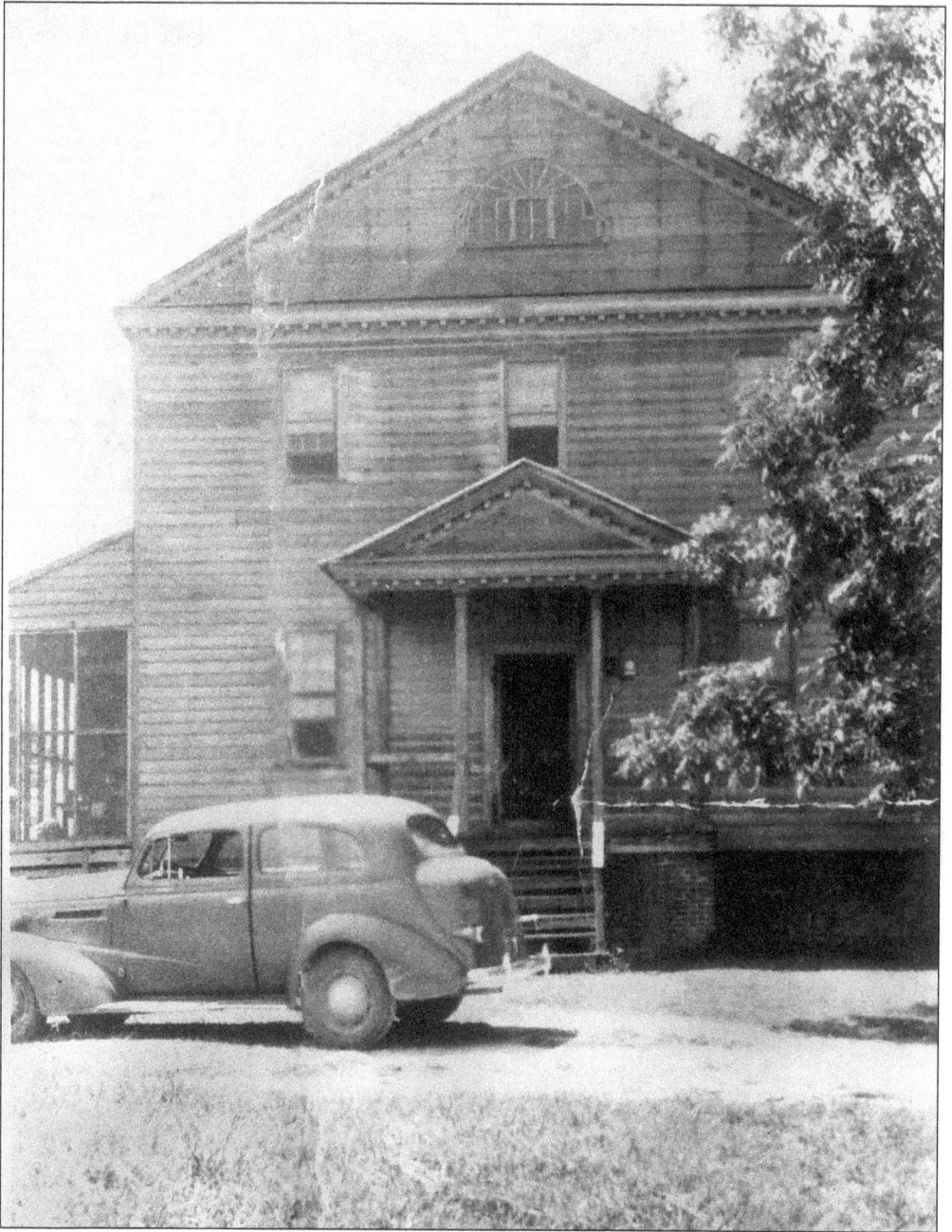

This is the Bond Plantation House, which is located off SR 1208, before Lin Bond's mother Emma Bond restored it in 1936. Emma had recently become a widow and it "took great courage for her to move back to her old home, which had no electric, plumbing or insulation," said her son Lin Bond. (Courtesy of Lin Bond.)

William E. "Winks" Bond (standing on the right side of tractor) watches driver Alex Stanley James Johnson (left) and an unidentified planter set tobacco plants in 1936. Lin and Amelia Bond now run this farm. (Photo by J.D. Griffen.)

The Bond family goes back several generations, is illustrated in this family reunion picture of 1997. From left to right are (front row) Lin Bond, Sherry Porter and children Walt Porter, John and Emily Layton, Yancey Bond, Beverly Bond, and Amelia Bond; (middle row) Bill Bond, Jewel Bond, Harriet Small, Lynne Layton, Emma Bond, Courtney Bond, and Sam Bond; (back row) Charles Small, Johnny Layton, Ed Small, and Winks Bond. (Courtesy of Amelia Bond; photo by Kermit Layton.)

The Robert W. Leary and Deborah Byrum Leary Home Place is seen in 1920. Shown from left to right are West Leary, Stillman Leary, Kate L. Boyce, Annie Bell L. Hollowell, and Bessie L Harrell. Sitting on the porch step is Deborah Byrum Leary (Courtesy of Ann Perry.)

According to Chowan County historian Walter Lane, Brownrigg-Dillard Grist Mill House at Small's Crossing was built around 1762. Walter started working at Dillard's Mill in 1940, and has continued for some 60 years. The original mill was destroyed in 1970, however a new motor-powered mill soon replaced it, and Walter still runs it. (Courtesy of Richard Dixon Jr.)

Kader Hoskins Harrell poses with his daughter Evelyn Harrell (at age two) outside his grocery store and gas station. The Hoskins Harrell store was located on Highway 32 South, near the Edenton Peanut Company, in 1934. (Courtesy of Penny Powell Binns.)

W.J. Webb owned a farm in Yeopin, where he and his father W.J. Webb Sr. raised a large cotton crop each year. (Courtesy of CCAC.)

This was the Zacheria Trotman Evans Country Store (*c.* 1926), located at the junction of Rocky Hock Road and Rocky Hock Landing Road. "Evans sold dry goods, groceries, hardware, gasoline, kerosene, and motor oil. He even had a barber shop in the rear," said Steve Evans, a great-grandson who lives in Rocky Hock. Z.T. Evans (1878–1949) also had a large farm, and he and his wife, Effie White Evans, raised 12 children. The boys on the store steps, from left to right, are Irvine Saunders, Ralph Saunders, and Roland Evans. (Courtesy of Steve Evans.)

This picture of Bessie Harrell Heath (1907–1986), soldier Joseph Linwood Harrell, and Sara Jane "Sallie" Harrell (1873–1961) was taken in front of June Lassiter's meat market on South Oakum Street in 1943. Joseph was home on leave before returning to the European war front. He was badly wounded in 1944, but recovered and returned home to live a productive life. (Courtesy of Evelyn Powell.)

Dr. John McMullan and his son John McMullan Jr. were "out for a spin" in their new Model T Ford in 1909. (Courtesy of HESHS.)

Back in 1932 a favorite pastime of the Kadar Hoskins Harrel family was to take a ride to town in their handsome luggage carriage. They posed for this interesting picture on East Church Street. From left to right are Kader Hoskins Harrell at the reins, Evelyn Harrell, and Patrica Harrell. (Courtesy of CCAC.)

Standing in front of Z.T. Evans's 1939 Chevrolet at the Home Place on Evans-Bass Road are, from left to right, (top photo, front row) Zackie Harrell, Jack Evans, Wallace Evans, and Merrill Evans; (top photo, back row) Carrol Evans (Aubrey) Harrell, Alvin Evans, and Wilbur Harrell; (bottom picture, front row) Effie and Zackeria Evans; (bottom picture, back row)Edward, Beulah, Lonia, Lillie, Alvin, Carey, Helen, Marvin, Pearl, Roland, Eleanor, and Milton. (Courtesy of Jack Evans)

Carey Moses Evans (1906–1985) and one of his children are plowing peppers on his Rocky Hock farm. His John Deere "La" was one of the first single row planting tractors in the area. (Courtesy of Jack Evans.)

In 1980 Mrs. Hazel Leary and her husband, West Leary of Leary Brothers Storage Company, received a blue ribbon award for their watermelon at the Chowan County Fair. Watermelons have been a major export crop for Chowan County for more than 100 years. Fine flavored melons known as Cowpen Neck Specials are grown along the Chowan River in the Cowpen Neck and Rocky Hock areas. (Courtesy of CCH.)

In 1942 the Byrum family celebrated the 85th birthday of their mother Tarrie. Seated from left to right are Arie Fury, Nannie Bell Byrum Privott (mother of group), Debra B. Leary, Mary Byrum Chappell (standing), and Thomas Campbell Byrum Sr.; sitting in front are Margaret Byrum Goodwin and daughter-in-law Lillian Forehand Byrum. (Courtesy of Corrine Thorud.)

Around 1930 the man with the pony called Pal arrived in Edenton to the children's delight. Posing in front of Dr. Murray Palmer Whichard's House, the children are, from left to right, Mary Forehand, Nick Gardner, Fannie Moore, and John Lester Forehand Jr. (at the reins). (Courtesy of Corrine Thorud.)

Nine

NOTABLE EVENTS
IN THE YEAR . . .

In the year 1889 the Edenton Agricultural and Fish Fair was held at the Edenton Fairground, which was located on the northeast corner of Broad and Freemason Streets. This location is now the site of Hicks Field. This field adjoins the John A. Holmes High School which was built in 1950. The main exhibit hall, a two-story octagonal building, was constructed by Theo Ralph. The fairground featured a racetrack with a gallery from which the elite could watch the races. The fair also had a fine Floral Hall and Domestic Pavilion. These buildings were replaced in 1915 by another set of buildings and the fair became known as the Chowan Fair. (Courtesy of SPML.)

In the year 1712 Christopher Gale became North Carolina's first chief justice. Gale (1680–1734) was born in New York, the son of Miles and Margaret Gale. He married Sarah Catherine Harvey, and came to North Carolina in 1700. In 1703 he was appointed a judge of the General Court of the colony. In 1707 he became the presiding justice of the court and served as a supreme court judge for several terms until his death in 1734. (Courtesy of NCDAH.)

In the year 1753, Samuel Johnson, who was born in Scotland, came to Edenton to study law with Thomas Barker. Johnson was the nephew of Royal Governor Gabriel Johnson. He was a Federalist delegate and was chosen president of the Hillsborough Convention in 1788. Johnson served as governor of North Carolina from 1787 to 1789. (Courtesy of NCDHA.)

112

In the year 1768 James Iredell Sr. (1751–1799) came to Eastern North Carolina from England. Iredell was appointed tax collector for the Port of Roanoke at 17, and he studied law under Samuel Johnson. Iredell was attorney general of North Carolina at age 28, and an associate justice of the Supreme Court at 39. As a Federalist delegate, Iredell fought hard for ratification of the 1798 constitution. (Courtesy of HESHS.)

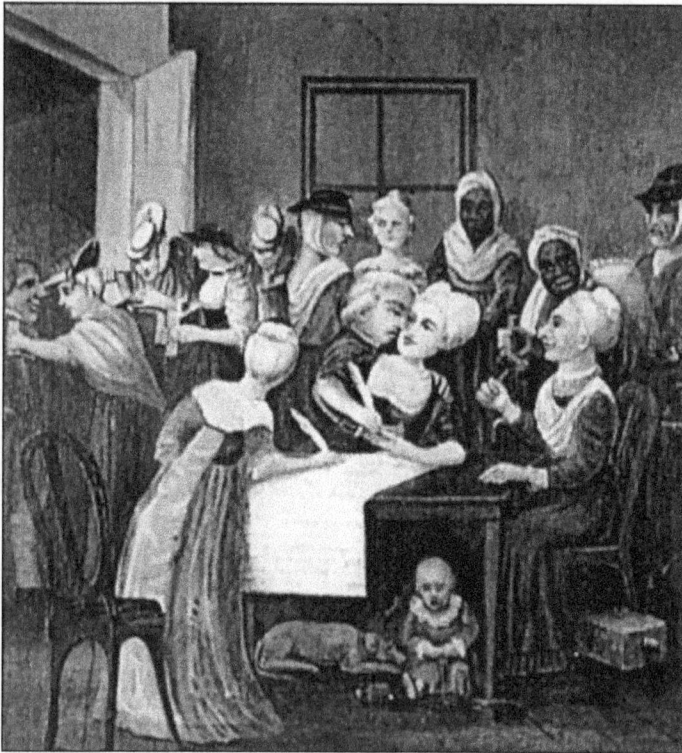

In the year 1774 Edenton's most notable event was illustrated in this English press cartoon, which depicts the Edenton Tea Party. This cartoon poked fun at Lord Bute, the advisor to King George III. Bute is shown staring at the lady holding the gavel. Bute, it has been said, was wrongly blamed for the English Stamp Act. (Courtesy of NCDHA.)

In the year 1775, John Paul Jones came to Edenton and appealed to Joseph Hewes to let him prove himself as a naval captain. When Hewes, a ship builder who was secretary of the Naval Affairs Committee of the Continental Congress, turned his ships over to the navy Jones was granted his commission. His naval record speaks for itself. As historian Rhodes put it, he was "the greatest fighting naval commander America ever had." (Courtesy of ECCC.)

In the year 1906, on November 20, James Wilson's body was exhumed from the Johnson family graveyard for reburial in Christ's Church Cemetery in Philadelphia. (Courtesy of HESHS.)

In the year 1908, on June 3rd a Confederate Reunion dance was held. Those attending were (front row) Josiah Harrell, A. Batevian, Andrew Briggs, W.D. Pruden, ? Holloman, Andrew J. Word, and W.D. Rea Potter; (second row) George A. Bowen, John Hollowell, Mrs. Tinisa Booham (widow of Capt. William Booham), and Abram T. Bush; (third row) John D. Parrish, Joel White, J.H. Deanes, Marliv Jones, T.D. Warren, Jeremiah Jones, J.H. Kiffs, W.A. Shepard, P.H. Bell, W.T. West, Arthur Collins and ? Cittism. (Courtesy of Frances Inglis and PSML.)

In the year 1916, on June 28, the North Carolina National Guard Regiment Company "I" marched down Magnolia Street (later renamed Eden Alley) to the N&SRR station to depart for training near the Mexican border. (Courtesy of CCAC.)

In the year 1927, on July 27, the wooden surfaced Chowan River Bridge was opened to traffic. Hundreds of cars poured across the new toll road to celebrate the opening. The Coast Guard cutter *Pamlico* stood off shore loaded with cheering passengers. Airplanes droned overhead, and two blimps flew so low their crews could talk to the crowd below. In Edenton flags were draped everywhere, and Broad Street was decorated as if to welcome a returning hero. The new bridge was 3 1/2 miles across, 22 feet wide, and had a 200-foot draw span. After 275 years of settlement, Bertie and Chowan counties were finally joined by a land connection, and were no longer dependent on a ferryboat crossing. Albert L. Roper, former mayor of Norfolk said, "the soul of a highway is its greater part. Highways are the arteries of a nation through which course the elements of friendliness and understanding." (Courtesy J.A. Mitchener III.)

In the year 1928, on March 31, a luncheon party was given at the Hinton Hotel in honor of Gov. A.M. McLean. The Hinton Hotel was built in 1926 on the site of the old Bayview Hotel at 109 East King Street, and was Edenton's first modern all-brick hotel. The Edenton News boasted "this hotel has 82 rooms, 78 with bath, and hot and cold water in every room." The Hinton was foreclosed in 1936 and operated as the Joseph Hewes Hotel until 1960, when Chowan County purchased and remodeled it for use as county offices. (Courtesy of HESHS.)

In the year 1937, on August 25, some 15,000 people listened as Rev. Robert B. Drane, D.D., said, "Today there is loosened the cord that has tied you to an age old isolation." The Albemarle Sound, a barrier that had shut off the "Lost Provinces" from the rest of the state had finally been conquered with the opening of the Albemarle Bridge. (Courtesy of J.A. Mitchener III.)

In the year 1943, this group of VIP's gathered for the opening of the Marine Corps Air Station. Standing from left to right are Dick Dixon, Judge Richard Dillard Dixon, Gov. Melville Broughton, Richard Reynolds Jr., and Julian Wood; (sitting) Louise Dixon, Alice Broughton, Mrs. Julian Wood, and Blitz Dillard Reynolds. (Courtesy of HESHS and CCH.)

In the year 1945, on August 24, the United States Navy occupied the United States Marine Corps Air Station east of Edenton. Built in 1943 on portions of the former Athol and Montpelier plantations, the base was operated by the Navy until the 1950s. This scene shows a morning muster in front of the administration building. (Courtesy of John Morehead.)

In the 1950s this Fire Prevention Week Parade down Broad Street was always led by the majorettes of the Edenton High School Band. (Courtesy of EFD.)

In the year 1965 the Edenton Town Council was sworn in at the old Municipal Building. From left to right are (front) George A. Byrum, J. Edwin Bufflap, and Luther Parks; (rear) William Privott (attorney), John A. Mitchner (mayor), J.D. Elliott (first ward councilman), Elton Forehand (third ward councilman), and Al Phillips (second ward councilman). (Courtesy of Pansy A. Elliott.)

In the year 1967 the annual celebration of the Edenton Woman's Club Pilgrimage was held at the Governor's Mansion in Raleigh. The club officers attended in colonial attire. Watching Mrs. Dan K. Moore sign the declaration are, from left to right, Mrs. Wood Privott, Mrs. Thomas Byrum, Mrs. J.D.Elliott, and Mrs. R.J. Boyce. (Courtesy of Pansy Elliott.)

In the year 1970 the Edenton Little Theater players presented *The Royal Gambit*, the story of Henry VIII and his six wives. The players were, from left to right, (top row) Jane Holmes, Gale Stevens, Corrine Throud, and Judy Earnhardt; (front row) Vivian P. Bond, Glenn Mabe as Henry the VIII, and Catherine Aman. (Courtesy of Corrine Thorud.)

In the year 1964–65, Chowan County Board of Commissioners, from left to right are William E. Bond (chairman), J. Clarence Leary, Bertha B. Bunch (clerk to the board), Dallas Jethro Jr., C.J. Hollowell, and Carey Evans. (Courtesy of Pansy Elliott.)

In the year 1991, the Edenton High School class of 1951 held their 40th reunion party. Shown from left to right are (first row) Gapie Daniels Whigham, Dorothy Baker Dalseq, Jean Jones Griffin, Evelyn Harrell Powell, Betty Letcher Manning, Dorine Alexander Privott, and Lucille Winslow Bartel; (second row) Virginia Copeland Garrett, Cynthia Ambrose Thebault, Betty Byrum Ward, Peggy Williams Norfleet, Jane Spry Weikel, and Hazel Braswell Lassiter; (third row) Robert White, Ray Spruill, Mack Privott, Billy Bond, Sherwood Chesson, and Bill Stallings; (fourth row) Byron Kehayes, Charlie Cannon, Haywood Rogerson, and Donald Campbell. (Courtesy of Evelyn Powell.)

In the year 1992, on November 24, the c. 1892 Zigler House at 108 North Broad Street was dedicated as the new home of the Historic Edenton Visitor Center. This gala event was attended, from left to right, by Wayne Goodwin (Chowan County Commissioner), Hon. R.M. "Pete" Thompson (NC House of Representatives), Hon. Vernon Jones (NC House of Representatives), Hon. Patric Dorsey (secretary, NC Dept. of Cultural Resources), Roy Harrell (Mayor of Edenton), Linda Jordon Eure (manager of the Historic Edenton State Historic Site), and Dr. William S. Prince Jr. (director, NC Division of Archives and History).

In the year 2001 the Emmrick Theater Production Company presented *Under His Wings* at the Rocky Hock Playhouse. This biblical love story of Ruth and Boaz was produced as a musical from the book of Ruth. Shown from left to right are (sitting) Gloria Emmrich and Donille Lester; (standing) Amanda Gallant, Yvonne Ozerities, Sharon Rosey, Gary Dop, Ben Emmrich, Mark Rash, Karie Wuerfelle, Julie Locke, and Mike Phillips. (Photo by Act One Ltd, 2001.)

ACKNOWLEDGMENTS

A pictorial history works well only if the people of the area being portrayed contribute their family and business pictures and their personal recollections. This book matured because many residents of Chowan County were so very cooperative. A very special effort on behalf of Chowan County was extended by Linda J. Eure, director of Historic Edenton State Historic Site, the Chowan Arts Council, the Chowan Herald, the Shepard-Pruden Memorial Library, and many Chowan County families, who were willing to share their photographic heritage with me. I found your stories very interesting, and your picture contributions are acknowledged by a credit line.

This book was completed without benefit of financial assistance. All expenses incurred were paid by the author.

INDEX

124

Holley, Butler,	85	Kiffs, J. H.	115	Manning, Betty Letcher	121
Holley, Mary H.	72	King, Elizabeth	31	Manning, James O.	67
Holley, Dr. O. L.	46	Kingsberry, R.I.,	85	Mansfield, Raymond	39,67
Holley, Phil,	78	Kirby, Shirley Toppin	59	Martin, Gary	90
Hollmart, Ella	78	Kramer's Garage.	47	Markham, Estelle	64
Holloman, Stella	86	Lackland, (unidentified)	90	Mason, Carlton	85
Holloman, W. D. Pruden	115	Lamb, Willie.	67	Mason, Clyde	67
Hollowell, Anne Bell L.	104	Lane, Betty Lou	75	Mathews, Bri-Anna	84
Hollowell, C.J.	67	Lane, Billy	88	Mayo, Rita	
Hollowell, Elizabeth	86	Lane, Hazel	88	90	
Hollowell, John	115	Lane, Walter	104	McMullan, John A. Jr.	119
Hollowell, Margaret	88	Lane, Wyane	88	McMullan, Dr. John Henry	57
Hollowell, Monissa	86	Langdale, Jackie	90	McMullan, John H., Jr.	45
Holly, Sawyer	83	Layton, Burt	78	McMullan, Phillip Sidney	93
Hoskins, Bessie	105	Layton, Emily	103	McMullan, Lina Tucker	57
Howard, Emily	64	Layton, Johnny	103	McNair, Joe	85
Hudson, Ethel	72	Layton, Lynne	103	Meredith, Rev. Thomas	67
Hudson Grace	90	Layton, Mary	78	Miller, Bailey	81
Huges, M.A.	44,67	Lassiter, Hazel Braswell	121	Mills, Snowden	39
Inglis, Francis	17	Lassiter, June	109	Mills, Walter	41
Iredell, James, Sr.	52,113	Lavezzo, John	89	Mitchener, Bessie Mae	61
Iredell, Hanna	52	Layton, Burt	78	Mitchener, John Agrippa	61
Israel, Bill,	67	Layton, Bertha	81	Mitchener, John A. Sr.	44
Jenkins, A.E.	67	Leary, Deborah Byrum	104,110	Mitchener, John A., III	43
Jernigan, Helen	90	Leary, Eulalia Hobbs	43	Mitchener, John, Sr.	43,44,45,50
Johnson, Amy	97	Leary, Evelyn	86	Mizelle, Wayne	49
Johnson, Annis.	83	Leary, Hazel Johnson	45,109	Monds, Arlese	86
Johnson, Charles	96	Leary, Ila	86	Mooney, Jack	67
Johnson, Cora Lee	84	Leary, J. Clarence	45	Moore, Fannie	110
Johnson, James C. Esq.	101	Leary, Josephine N.	32	Moore, Mrs. Dan K.	120
Johnson, Lula	72,83	Leary, Julius Craig	43,86	Moore, Lee.	67
Johnson, Samuel	77,112,113	Leary, Leon,	67	Moore, Virginia C.	64
Jones, Beatrice	72	Leary, Lillian Webb	45,90	Morain, Elizabeth	64
Jones, Danny	89	Leary, R. West	45,50,67,104,109	Morgan, Ashton	90
Jones, Jeremiah	115	Leary, Shelia	75	Morgan, Charles	0
Jones, John	90	Leary, Stillman,	104	Morgan, Lesslie	85
Jones, John Paul	114	Leary, Dr. William J., Sr.	33,51	Morris, Louvennia	76
Jones, Lena	86	Leggett, Dr. Walter A.	80	Morris, Ruth	76
Jones, Marliv	115	Lester,Donille	123	Murdough, Van Dora	83
Jones, Meridith	85	Lewis, Mary Hester.	86	Muth, Jacob	44
Jones, Rodney	67	Lindsay, Tex	67	New, Virginia	86
Jones Spec	50	Littlejohn, William	58	Newey, Anne	84
Jones, Hon. Vernon	122	Littlejohn, Sara Blount	58	Newsome, B. C.	82
Jordan, Adelia	62	Lip, Fannie	86	Nichols, Emma	84
Jordan, Ann	89	Long, Joseph	85	Nixon, Billy	88
Jordan, Jacob	88	Long, Ruby Buncn	75	Nixon, Celia Rae	76
Jordan, Marshall	47	Longdale, Marie	86	Nixon, Jeanette	75
Jordan, Sylvia	89	Lupton, Harold J.	49	Nixon, Martha	81
Joyner, Millard	88	Luten, Thomas	100	Nixon, Mary	81
Joyner, Rosa, B.	72,73	Mabe, Glenn	121	Nixon, Roy	75
Katkaveck, Frankie	89	Mack, George	60	Norcom, Dr. Thomas	99
Kehayes, Byron	121	Mackey's Ferry	18,19	Norcom, Dr. William	99